In The Presence of Mine Enemies

A GUIDEPOSTS 2-IN-1 SELECTION

Life More Abundant

In The ★ Presence of Mine Enemies

Howard and Phyllis Rutledge
with Mel and Lyla White

Life More Abundant

Charles L. Allen

GUIDEPOSTS ASSOCIATES, INC. Carmel, New York

About these books

It is hard to imagine a better combination of spiritual adventure and practical help than this Guideposts selection, another in our 2-in-1 series. The first book is one of the most dramatic stories of faith to come out of the Vietnam war; the second is an inspiring art of living book focusing on everyday problems we all face again and again.

Husband and wife Howard and Phyllis Rutledge tell about their seven-year-long Vietnam ordeal in the first half of this volume fittingly titled *In the Presence of Mine Enemies*. And what a fascinating account it is of two people trying to deal with life shredding problems. Alone, neither would have been able to cope with them, but both Howard in an Hanoi prison and Phyllis in San Diego find a spiritual reserve greater than either had ever imagined. This is especially true of Howard, a career pilot in the Navy, strong successful, self-confident. In fact, like so many, his life had evolved to the point where he found little need of the faith he had been steeped in as a child. He was too busy. But then after his plane was shot down and he was imprisoned, he found mountains of time and a physical and emotional testing so great that he turned to the only One left, and to his amazement that One was still by his side and still willing to respond. Wife Phyllis, meanwhile, went through a different kind of Job-like testing in California.

Poignantly, she recalls what it was like for the family of one missing in action. For five long years she and her children lived in a gray world between hope and despair, not knowing whether the head of their house was dead or alive. She, too, calls upon God to guide and sustain her. Mrs. Rutledge's role is no less heroic than her husband's as she deals with personal tragedy on the home front. Together, on opposite sides of the world, they are bound by an invisible reality which transcends miles, time, doubts, fear. It is a magnificent story, not about war or hate or political systems, but about love—God's love, which is never more real than in this moving book.

The second Guideposts selection is another of Charles Allen's best-selling books, *Life More Abundant*. Twice before, Guideposts readers have been offered Dr. Allen's books—*God's Psychiatry* and *All Things Are Possible Through Prayer*—and in that same tradition this book is a storehouse of faith-building principles.

Over a million copies of this popular minister's many books have been sold and only a brief sampling from one of them will explain why. Dr. Allen deals with the problems we all face, whether they be large life-and-death struggles or smaller, thorn-in-the-side annoyances which detract and steal the blood from the abundant life God wants for us. This book, like those which have gone before, offers practical, specific help for defeating your problems. The essence of Dr. Allen's message is unchanging: Through Jesus Christ there is help for any need you have. Illness, loneliness, poverty, doubt, worry, bereavement, whatever—Dr. Allen has fresh insight, helpful counsel for you.

Like the book which precedes it, *Life More Abundant* promises and delivers Good News to all believers. We believe you will receive a rich spiritual blessing from both of these exciting books.

The Editors

In The ★ Presence of Mine Enemies

Howard and Phyllis Rutledge
with Mel and Lyla White

Illustrations by Gerald Coffee

FLEMING H. REVELL COMPANY
Old Tappan, New Jersey

To all who never stopped hoping and praying for
our return, and to God who answered those prayers.

Contents

1   Shot Down and Captured 1
2   Missing In Action 10
3   My First Interrogation 13
4   Despair 22
5   The Routine 24
6   More Torture 34
7   More Grief 44
8   My First Roommate 48
9   The Alcatraz Gang 58
10 Another Tragedy 66
11 New Hope 69
12 Word After Five Years 78
13 Camp Unity 83
14 Help For John 95
15 Going Home 99
16 "Hello, Phyllis?" 107
17 After Seven Years 113
18 Some Resolutions 116
19 Reunion 120

I

Shot Down and Captured

Howard Rutledge
North Vietnam
November 28, 1965

I was the Executive Officer of Fighter Squadron 191 aboard the attack Carrier USS *Bon Homme Richard* in the Gulf of Tonkin, and we were conducting round-the-clock missions over North Vietnam. This day I was a flight leader in a large force of fighter and attack aircraft. Our mission was to destroy a strategic bridge just northwest of Thanh Hoa. My F-8 Crusader jet, armed with two 2,000 lb. bombs, two-air-to-air missiles, and four 20mm cannons, had catapulted from the carrier, rendezvoused with the squadron, refueled in the air, and approached the target as planned.

As I crossed from the safety of the sea to the enemy beaches, I signaled FEET DRY to the pilots of my flight and reported the overcast weather conditions to the strike leader. At almost 600 mph I broke through the haze at 5,000 feet and off to my right got a clear view of our target.

We suspected the area might be heavily protected and immediately I faced a fierce barrage of antiaircraft fire. I could see the guns below belching flame and knew that shells were exploding all around me; but after 200 safe missions over Korea and North and South Vietnam, the thought of

I

being hit never crossed my mind.

As I approached the roll-in point for my drop, two anti-aircraft shells exploded somewhere in the tail section behind me. The pilot of a Crusader fighter sits right in the nose and cannot really see the fuselage aft. Because the plane responded satisfactorily and because I would be headed toward the safety of the sea at the end of the bombing run, I selected my afterburner and continued my attack on the target almost at the speed of sound. I dropped my bombs, and, still accelerating, turned to a heading toward the sea.

It was then my fighter received another hit. This time I knew it was a mortal blow. The plane pitched down about 20° and commenced an uncontrollable roll to the left.

I hear my wingman on the radio, "They are really shooting in here!"

I tried a quick transmission in reply, "I am hit! I am hit and bailing out!"

The plane was traveling like lightning and rolling uncontrollably. The stick went dead in my hands. The horizon spun past. We rolled 360°, and a few degrees before top-dead center I jerked at the ejection curtain. My escape seat hurled into the air as another shell burst under the cockpit itself. A fragment tore into my leg. I made one 360° tumble and saw the horizon pass. The chute deployed automatically, and I watched with horror as my plane exploded into a ball of flame before me.

If I had waited another second to eject, I would have died in that explosion of bombs, jet fuel, and cannon shells. My grateful reveries were interrupted by a new danger.

Remember how bullets zing past the good guys in B-grade television westerns and old war movies? I could hear bullets singing past me and could see the holes they were making in my parachute. Instinctively, I hung limp in the

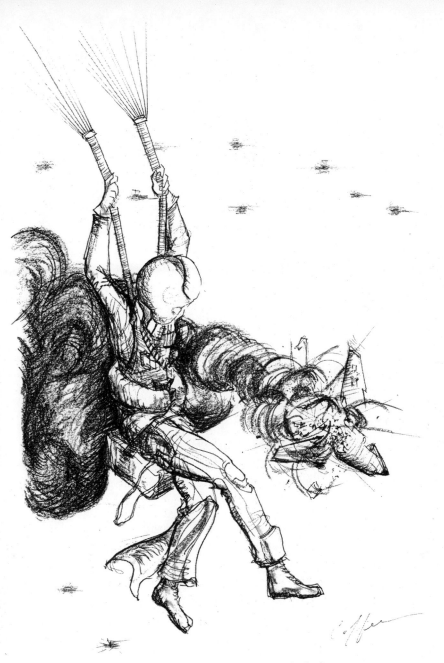

I watched with horror as my plane exploded
into a ball of flame before me.

shrouds to make the enemy believe I had been mortally wounded. Still curious to see who could be firing, I cracked open my eyes, slowly turned my head downwards and, to my horror, discovered I was descending rapidly into the town square of a rather large village. A crowd was gathering. Everyone was gesturing in my direction, and I could hear them shouting excitedly.

Resurrected by the sight, I reached up and pulled the two front risers that altered my course and sent me drifting faster toward the flooded rice fields at the edge of town, and away from the welcoming committee that was forming there.

I had never parachuted from a plane before that day, and though it all seemed terribly unreal, I was functioning on instinct carefully trained into me by the U.S. Navy survival schools. In the last few seconds of descent, I could see that I was going to land about twenty yards to the north of a huge dike that ran east and west to the sea. For a navy pilot, the sea is friendly. I was hoping that those big, beautiful, search-and-rescue helicopters had been notified of my plight and were on their way to lift me back to safety. I had seen my wingman, Lt. Ken Masat, risk his own life to circle through the antiaircraft fire to check out my chute and get a sighting on my descent. He would notify them. If I could just stay free long enough to reach the dike and run for the sea, they would find me. But already I could count perhaps fifty men running in my direction. I landed standing up. Fortunately, I was knee-deep in mud; without that my legs would have broken almost certainly. Instinctively, I released my lower rocket fittings to get rid of the raft and survival paraphernalia. One release rocket wouldn't fire, and I struggled desperately to free myself.

By now I could hear voices shouting from all sides. In the two minutes it took to break free, only one young Vietnamese militiaman had gotten between me and that important dike.

He was in his early twenties and carried a machete which he waved threateningly. Yelling at the top of his voice, he ran toward me, blocking my escape to the sea.

I jerked my 38 revolver from my survival gear, pulled back the hammer and pointed it at his chest, hoping to frighten him away. He didn't waver. Still screaming and wielding the machete high over his head, he ran to point-blank range. I pulled the trigger, and he fell dead at my feet. I will never forget the look on his face as he slumped forward or my own horror as he fell. By now, a large crowd was running toward me from every direction. There were no military weapons on these farmer-militiamen, but they carried knives, long, sharp-pointed sticks, and machetes wired to poles prepared for just such an occasion. Everyone was shouting in a cacophony of Vietnamese curses and threats. They stopped about fifteen feet from me and formed a ring, completely blocking my escape. They could see the young man in the water at my feet and were afraid to come any closer. I circled, aiming my gun towards each man as I turned. We were at a strange impasse—each eyeing the other—each afraid.

Perhaps a minute passed. During those long seconds, I realized this was going to be my final appearance on the earth. It was perhaps the first time I had seriously contemplated death. Then an old, gray-haired Vietnamese stepped out from the ring.

I bore down on him with the 38. He dropped his machete and put his arms down at his side. Then he raised them for silence. The crowd obeyed and an eerie silence followed. The next two minutes were critical for me. I couldn't speak Vietnamese; he couldn't speak English. But through gestures and signs, he promised me that if I would not shoot again, he, their leader, would guarantee my safety.

To this day I cannot believe that those few wild gestures

could make that complex message clear.

Realizing that to trust the old man was the best of some very bad options, I threw my five remaining shells as far as I could in one direction and the revolver in the other. If they were going to kill me, it wouldn't be with my survival weapon.

Then, the brief silence was broken by a unison scream of revenge, and the crowd was on me. They pounded me to my knees. I felt a shower of blows on my head and shoulders from their bamboo clubs. Each man and boy, feeling years of pent-up anger and hatred, took this moment of revenge. Each got his blow, and for a moment I feared that I had made the wrong decision. I had been deceived. Then—just before unconsciousness—the old man intervened. The blows and kicks and curses ceased, and I was dragged to my feet.

At that moment the village commissar arrived, wielding a vintage German luger. His was the first uniform I had seen that day, and he was obviously in charge. He took one arm, the old man took the other, and together they half-dragged, half-walked me toward the village. In the confusion a boy about twelve years old slipped out of the crowd, deftly lifted my watch right off my arm and ran off with it. Later in the crowd I saw him passing out the twenty-dollar bills I had been carrying in my flight jacket. He had no idea how much those green bills were worth.

The crowd was jubilant. They had captured a valuable prisoner. They were returning to their village in triumph. Suddenly, I felt afraid. Everyone was looking toward the village. Instinctively, I looked backward and saw, to my horror, a man, his face twisted in anger, running towards me. A huge scar ran down the right side of his face; his right eye was missing; he was running at me full-tilt, carrying a three-foot-long rusty harpoon. He had every intention of planting that lance deep into my back. I lunged in front of the commissar who, upon realizing my predicament, felled the man with one strong blow to the face with that old German luger.

By now we had crossed to the edge of the village. The whole town had gathered. For a moment they just stood and looked at this strange man from another world. They were peasants dressed uniformly in simple, black, pajama outfits. I stood before them in full-battle dress, armed with a flare gun, sheath knives, a two-way radio, life vest, compass, navigational watch, and miscellaneous survival paraphernalia. I must have looked like a man from the moon to them. For one long moment we stood in open-mouthed unbelief seeing each other close up for the first time. Then they laid me spread-eagle on the dirt path and commenced to undress me and relieve me of my treasures.

They didn't use any of the zippers on my flight clothing. They took knives and machetes and cut off everything, including my boots. In seconds I was completely naked. Someone tossed me short, ragged pants and a child's short-sleeved shirt with no buttons. I struggled into my new uniform and sat back exhausted on a low rock wall, wiped my arm across my face and was quite surprised when it came back covered with blood. I must have been a sight, almost naked, covered with mud, beaten to a pulp, my leg wounded and bleeding.

The commissar held the crowd back, unsure what to do with his unexpected prize. Then the crowd parted and a little Vietnamese man approached carrying a black medic bag. A woman followed with a basin of water. Together they washed my wounds, wrapped a bandage around my head, and gave me a shot in each arm. I recognized the syringe of morphine from my survival gear and supposed the other was a tetanus shot. This moment of compassion probably saved my life. These people had every reason to hate me.

7

If it hadn't been for the commissar, I believe they would have killed me on the spot. This medic went about his work without a smile or friendly gesture as if compelled by a force of compassion that outweighed any hatred and desire for revenge.

When the medic finished his hasty repairs, the commissar dragged me through the crowd to a little shelter just off the central village square. I lay on my back on a hard, wooden pallet on the dirt floor. The room was dark, with no windows; a kerosene lamp burned nearby, lighting the room in flickering semi-darkness. All afternoon and into the night the commissar let the villagers enter the room in groups of three or four. No one showed particular hostility. They were mainly curious. No one did me any harm. Now and then a teen-ager would spit on me, say something in anger, and punch me with his finger, I suppose to tell his young friends he had touched the fallen American pilot. Few tried to speak. Most simply looked, then hurried on. I thought of funerals back in Tulsa and how mourners approached the casket, stared for a moment, and then walked on. This time the corpse stared back. Then the crowds stopped coming. I was alone for the first time since my capture. Reviewing the events of the day made me aware of one thing: It was a miracle that I was alive. I had not thought about God much since dropping out of Sunday school in my late teens, but lying on the floor, I could not help but think of Him then.

I had come close to death so many times in that one day and each time I had felt the hand of God. Pictures flooded my mind: the plane exploding into a ball of flame moments after I had ejected—shots zinging by me, making holes in my parachute—the crowd of angry men beating and kicking me, intent upon my death—that unforgettable face twisted by anger and by war, running at me with the rusty lance— the medic—the commissar—the old man.

I was a prisoner of war. I had no idea what my fate would be, but the Lord had made Himself abundantly clear. He was there with me in the presence of my enemies, and I breathed a prayer of thanks.

2

Missing in Action

Phyllis Rutledge
San Diego, California,
November 28, 1965

It was Sunday and my four young children and I worshiped together in the Clairemont First Southern Baptist Church of San Diego. No one remembers what happened in the service that day, but we had been inspired by the music and by the Reverend Charles W. Foley's sermon. We stopped at a supermarket nearby to pick up some groceries. The children unloaded the trunk and were already in the house when our friends Jack Snyder and Merle Gorder drove into the driveway beside me. I didn't think anything strange about their visit until I saw the navy chaplain getting out of the back seat and walking toward me. Then I knew instantly. Howard was dead!

"No, no, no," I said, over and over, denying what I feared the most. I didn't faint, but my knees did give way. Immediately Merle had his arm around me, guiding me towards the house.

My tears began to flow. I wanted to be brave, a stoic navy wife, a Christian saint, but the tears came anyway. For a while there seemed to be no end of crying. As we walked in the back door, Merle was trying to comfort me.

"No, it's not that bad, Phyllis. We think he's all right. His wingman saw a chute before the plane exploded."

Inside the back door my oldest daughter Sondra, fifteen, approached and put her arm around me. The look in her face told me that she knew. There was no need to explain. My tears kept falling. I wanted to stop and gather the family around. I wanted to explain calmly and quietly that Daddy had been shot down and was missing in action, but no words came. The older children knew without being told. John, twelve, disappeared immediately into his bedroom, and Peggy, seven, and Barbara, six were too young to really understand.

Soon, Merle's wife Kay and Jennie Speer, another family friend, dropped by. Within minutes it seemed the house was filled with people. Pastor Foley was there and folks from the church, navy friends and neighbors. Their eyes were wet, their faces reflected how deeply they shared our anguish.

As if walking in a daze, I found myself fixing refreshments, making coffee and hopeful conversation with my friends and neighbors. I was in a state of shock, answering the door, putting flowers into vases, thanking people for their concern, and somehow carrying on.

I was too busy to notice that John had not come out of his room. He was all alone in there and really suffering. Until the last few years, John had felt his dad had always favored the girls in our family. Recently, through their common interest in Little League, John and his dad had become good friends. Now, his father was missing in action. In my preoccupation with the house filled with company, I never went near his bedroom door, and still, today, deeply regret letting him face his sadness alone.

The crowd of friends, the noisy kitchen, the little girls playing at my feet made it seem almost like any other day. Then the sun went down. My body began to ache with tiredness but my dear, thoughtful friends just would not go away. I wanted desperately to be alone, to have a moment by myself to think it through. Then, at last they were gone. The kids were asleep. I walked into our bedroom and slumped down on the bed.

The first thing I noticed was Howard's picture smiling down on me. I took the picture off the wall and held it close asking all those endless questions countless military wives have always asked.

Is he alive? Is he lying wounded somewhere in the jungle? Was he captured, even executed, or is he locked up already in an enemy prison somewhere? Will he survive?

Looking into the dark brown eyes on that photograph, I knew Howard was in the hands of God. There was nothing I could do about him but hope and pray. The real question to face now was how could we survive? In the rooms nearby were four young children who needed a father's love and attention. In the bedroom file were piles of papers, insurance policies, wills and records I could not begin to understand. In my kitchen desk were all the bills accumulating in his absence that he could straighten out in one long frantic evening when he returned. But now he wasn't coming back. I had to face those problems alone.

Being alone was nothing new. The career military wife spends a large part of her life alone. When Sondra was born, Howard was practicing jet landings on a carrier somewhere in the Pacific. When John was born, Howard was standing watch for a good friend whose basement had been flooded. When Peggy was born, my husband was stationed on a ship deployed in the Mediterranean. I've spent half my life—or so it seemed that night—waiting for him to come home and straighten out the messes I had made. Now, I didn't have a husband to take care of me or my messes. This time he wasn't coming home.

My First Interrogation

3

Howard Rutledge
New Guy Village, Hanoi,
November 29, 1965

My first day in captivity had left me exhausted but grateful to be alive. I had survived the day on grace and my adrenalin. Now, the adrenalin was wearing off, and the morphine was taking hold. My thoughts slowed to a halt, and I floated in a drugged stupor on the floor of that village shelter. A loud commotion in the village square jolted me back to my senses. It was the sound of a crowd of cheering peasants running along behind a large truck. The truck stopped.

The door burst open, and in marched eight or nine North Vietnamese regular soldiers in army uniforms. They hauled me to my feet. It was then I learned my badly sprained leg could not support my weight, so the soldiers dragged me between them through the crowd outside. There were no electric lights in the village, but makeshift torches lit the night. The people cheered the soldiers as they loaded me onto the back of a half-ton military truck. I lay spread-eagle on the slats, while one young soldier blindfolded me and lay a tarpaulin over my shivering body. Unfortunately, the tarpaulin wasn't meant for warmth but to guarantee that

13

I could not see anything on the coming journey.

The truck pulled out of that village and sped toward Hanoi. We drove the entire night on a very rough road, stopping every few hours for the soldiers to unveil me to another cluster of applauding peasants carrying torches and cheering the soldiers loudly. One particular stop was unforgettable. There were no crowds this time; in fact, we were parked on a pontoon bridge in the middle of a wide river. The soldiers took off my blindfold and pointed thirty feet above me to the Ham Rong bridge which they thought had been my target. It was still standing. I noticed that our truck's wheels were submerged beneath the water and that the pontoon bridge was totally hidden from the surface to camouflage it. My enemy was proud, and boisterous, and confident.

At about dawn the next morning, I could hear traffic and the sounds of a city. The truck stopped and my blindfold was removed; then, we drove into a large fortress in the heart of Hanoi. In the few seconds I had to survey my surroundings, it was perfectly clear that this was a prison that would permit no escape.

A series of huge concrete walls fifteen to twenty feet high surrounded the inner buildings. Broken glass was cemented into the surface, and hot, electric wires ran the length of the walls. There was a dry moat around the prison separating one tall wall from the other.

We drove through iron gates and stopped before an ominous structure of concrete brick and motar approximately thirty-five feet long and twenty-five feet wide. Inside his tomblike building were eight individual cells, 6 x 6 feet. Each held two concrete bunks, one on each side, with barely enough room to walk between them. The bunks were about two feet wide and at the bottom of each, imbedded in cement, was a set of iron stocks. A prisoner would put his feet in place, and another iron bar was forced down across the top with an iron pin to lock them. There were seven cells with an eighth prepared as a kind of washing place. This was Heartbreak Hotel. It was one of many cell blocks of the huge Hoa Lo prison complex. Built by the French early in the century, American aircrews housed there had nicknamed the prison the "Hanoi Hilton." Needless to say, this was no hotel.

I saw no other prisoners as I was dragged into Cell 7. Only minutes passed before the guards moved me again from Heartbreak Hotel into a completely different section of the prison. Later I learned my second stop was nicknamed New Guy Village, for almost every new prisoner was housed temporarily in its cells.

The retaining room I now found myself in had knobby plaster walls that gave the place a cavelike appearance. Nicknamed the "Knobby Room," it was small and the filthiest place I had seen to date. It was like the worst of slums in miniature. I sat down on a pile of debris in the center of this mess and took stock of my condition.

I had no clothes. I was freezing cold. I had eaten nothing for twenty-four exhausting hours. My body ached. My leg and wrist were sprained and swelling badly. I was covered with caked blood and filth. The officers' quarters on the *Bon Homme Richard,* a warm bath, a hot cup of coffee, that emergency first-aid kit I hadn't opened in ten years seemed a million miles away.

No sooner had I begun to collect my thoughts than I was interrupted by a burly Vietnamese officer who led me from the Knobby Room into an interrogation center nearby. I knew this moment was coming. I had been trained in survival school and was well versed in the Code of Conduct. I was to answer only four questions. The questions began almost politely.

"Your name?"

"Howard Rutledge," I answered, teeth chattering in the morning chill.

"Your rank and serial number ?" he continued.

"Commander; 506435," I replied.

"Your date of birth ?"

"13 November 1928."

The questions continued without pause. "Your squadron and ship ?"

I refused to answer further, explaining the American fighting man's code and the Internationl Conventions at Geneva, 1949.

His reply was calm and quiet. "You are not a prisoner of war," he said. "Your government has not declared war upon the Vietnamese people. You must answer my questions. You are protected by no international law." I continued to refuse to answer any of his questions.

Suddenly, the interrogator closed his notebook, leaned over toward me and said, "Commander Rutledge, you are a criminal, guilty of high crimes against the Vietnamese people. If you do not answer my questions, you will be severely punished."

With that I was led back into the Knobby Room and given thirty minutes to decide. The guard returned, and I was taken back into the interrogation room and asked the first four questions, which I answered again. The fifth I refused to answer. I was threatened again and returned to the Knobby Room. This little charade happened every thirty minutes for the entire day. The verbal lashings increased each time I refused to cooperate. But every time I returned to the Knobby Room, I felt I had beaten them again.

Meanwhile my body ached with growing ferocity. I had received no clothing, and I was beginning to "cold soak." My body temperature was dropping to the temperature of the North Vietnamese winter evening; my swollen wrist and leg were throbbing, but I was going to win. Survival school had taught me well. Again I was called to the interrogation room.

This time when I refused to answer the threat of punishment sounded like a promise. "Now, Commander Rutledge," the interrogator said, "you will be severely punished."

I was taken back to the Knobby Room. The officer who spoke English was joined by a guard we named Pigeye and three men in civilian clothes. Pigeye probably tortured more Americans than any other North Vietnamese. The others looked like criminals off the street. A guard with a burp gun closed the door on the six of us and stood watching through the bars.

The officer told me to sit on the floor and extend my legs straight out. My left leg was so badly swollen that I could not straighten it, so one of the interrogator's accomplices planted his heavy boot on my knee and forced the swollen leg onto the cement floor. I felt a flash of pain and simultaneously felt my leg pop. That guard probably did me a real favor by forcing into place my badly dislocated leg. It may seem strange to thank God for this sadistic act, but I don't know what would have happened to my leg if that guard hadn't acted.

Then they forced my legs into spurlike shackles and used a pipe and strong rope to lock both ankles firmly into place. Next they forced my arms into a long-sleeved shirt and began to tie them behind me from above my elbows to my wrists. One guard put his foot on my back, forcing the laces tight enough to cut off all circulation and pulling my shoulder blades almost apart. I could see the rope cut through my wrists all the way to the bone, but they did not bleed, because the bindings acted like a tourniquet cutting off circulation entirely into my arms and hands.

I began to have severe pains in my arms; by forcing myself on my side, I could see my arms and hands had turned a deep shade of blue. It slowly dawned on me that they were going to leave me in this miserable position until I answered their questions. For a while I thought that I would die. I never prayed for death, but I did pray for unconsciousness. For a least three hours I lay in his position, my prayer unanswered.

Then the guards returned, unlaced my arms and legs, and left again. I had a terrible fear that my arms would never function normally, but an hour or so later feeling began to return, and except for deep cuts and bruises they soon moved quite normally. My first contact with torture as a weapon of war had left me a bit unnerved, and when they brought me once again to the interrogation room, it took all the strength I could muster to refuse to answer their questions once again.

All they wanted was for me to answer question number five—my squadron, airwing, and ship. If I didn't answer, I would be hogtied again and probably lose the use of my arms and hands, if not my life.

"Commander Rutledge, you have committed high crimes against our people. You will be severely punished if you do not answer our questions."

My explanation was interrupted; I was returned to the Knobby Room, placed in shackles, tightly bound, and left again to ponder my resistance. This time the guards slapped me several times before they left. And each time during the night, as I refused to answer, their blows increased. Around dawn the interrogator was relieved by a high-ranking officer. Later I learned the prisoners called him Colonel Nam.

I had been through an entire night of punishment, and the more I had refused, the more angry and impatient everyone had become. Now, everyone was tense and angry. When Colonel Nam repeated the questions and then the

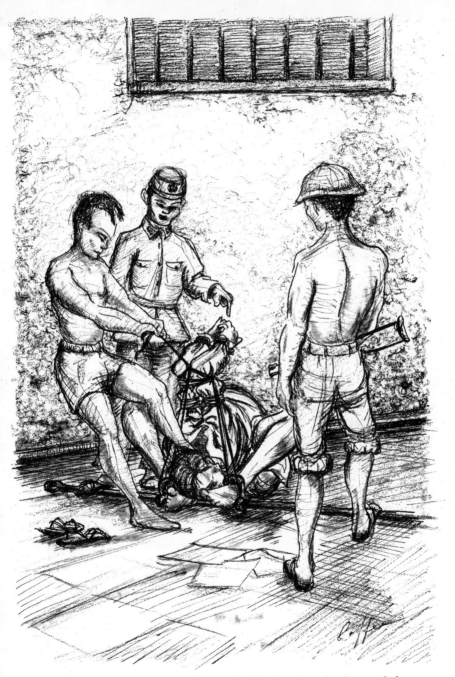

One guard put his foot on my back, forcing the laces tight enough to cut off all circulation and pulling my shoulder blades almost apart.

threats, I exploded in anger.

"Why don't you go ahead and kill me, because I will *not* answer your questions!" Colonel Nam did not reply. He just watched as the guards dragged me away. This time they would have their answers.

I was shackled; the laces were pulled unbearably tight. I had not eaten for two days, and my requests for medical care for my wrist and legs and head were ignored. I had not even been permitted to have a normal kidney or bowel movement in the entire time. I still had no clothes and was truly cold.

This time they laced the rope from my ankles up around my neck through my handcuffed wrists. This forced me into a pretzel-like position; if I bent forward or leaned backward, the rope would choke me. I had to sit in a perfectly upright position, with arms laced tightly behind my back. One guard repeatedly struck my head and shoulders with a bamboo pole; another jumped up and down on the rope binding my legs, cutting deep into my ankles. I prayed for unconsciousness. I asked God to give me strength. I thought about my wife Phyllis and my family, and knew I would never see them again. I knew my ability to endure any more physical or mental pain was rapidly ending. I determined that before I cracked completely, I would volunteer to answer their questions, hoping that while I still had some control, I could lie and deceive them and so survive.

"Stop." My voice was no more than a whisper. "I will answer."

Immediately, they undid my bindings and unshackled me. As I lay there on the floor, the interrogator entered and politely asked me question number five.

"What is your service?" he said.

"The United States Navy," I replied.

Then he was gone. They had their fifth answer. It was all

they wanted to know.

Guards brought a blanket and a suit of long prison clothes. At last I was allowed to relieve myself. I could not eat. I received no medical attention, not even Mercurochrome, but I lay back on that concrete slab and slept.

4

Despair

Phyllis Rutledge
San Diego, California,
November 29, 1965

The morning after we learned that Howard had been shot down over North Vietnam we all made brave attempts to go on living. I fixed the children breakfast and sent them to school. I put on the coffeepot, sat down to read the morning paper, and the headlines shouted out the news again.

LOCAL NAVY PILOT—MISSING IN ACTION

For the third time in less than twenty-four hours, I was crying. To be honest, I wasn't crying only for Howard. I was also crying for Howard's wife—me. I felt lonely and deserted and afraid I wouldn't be able to handle those next long days ahead.

Then I remembered the night only eight weeks before when Howard sat me down on our bed, took out a household ledger from his briefcase and a whole notebook of instructions. Patiently, he told me how to pay bills, insurance premiums, car payments, and the like. It probably sounds silly, but this was one of the most beautiful nights of our marriage, sitting on our bed at midnight with papers spread in all directions, talking business. For the first time in our life together, he had really sat down to share all these things with me.

Maybe he had a premonition. His squadron had been flying round-the-clock missions over North Vietnam. Several of his friends had been killed or captured. Three days before, his father had died and Howard had been forced to think of death and those whom death left behind. Apparently, Howard was trying to prepare me.

The next morning he flew to Travis Air Force Base and took a trans-Pacific flight to catch his ship. Now he was gone, and I had the ledger.

It's hard to be the head of a household with no real preparation. I started dating Howard when I was just fourteen, and he was a senior in high school. Dependence set in early. He made almost all the decisions. Even when he was stationed on a ship halfway round the world, I knew I could call him or write a letter and ask how to handle this or settle that. Now he couldn't tell me what to do. I was on my own.

5

The Routine

Howard Rutledge
Heartbreak Hotel, Hanoi,
December, 1965

On the morning of December 1, two guards roused me from
a fitful sleep and marched me out of New Guy Village across
the prison into Cell 2, Heartbreak Hotel. When the door
slammed and the key turned in that rusty, iron lock, a feeling
of utter loneliness swept over me. I lay down on that cold
cement slab in my 6 x 6 prison. The smell of human excrement burned my nostrils. A rat, large as a small cat, scam-
pered across the slab beside me. The walls and floors and
ceilings were caked with filth. Bars covered a tiny window
high above the door. I was cold and hungry; my body ached
from the swollen joints and sprained muscles.

I felt guilty for having answered more. Worst of all, I
felt totally alone. I seldom cry, but that day tears of self-pity
and of fear welled up in my eyes, and I fought them back.
This was my first taste of solitary confinement. The war
against my nerves had begun.

Then I heard a voice.

"New guy that just moved in, what's your name? What
ship are you from?"

I literally sprang to that window and pressed my face

against the cold iron bars. Down the narrow passageway staring back at me were other Americans. Commander James Stockdale, airwing commander downed in September had spoken. I was not alone!

At great personal risk he briefed me quickly and clearly about the other men in Heartbreak. In a cell across the way was Commander Harry Jenkins, a squadron commander in Airwing 16. To the left was Air Force Captain George McNight, downed only weeks before. In Cell 4 was Lt. Comdr. Duffy Hutton from a photo-recon squadron, and across from him Marine Captain Harley Chapman off the attack carrier USS *Oriskany,* and Air Force Lt. Jerry Singleton, a helicopter pilot downed in November.

In quiet, rapid phrases, Commander Stockdale told me that to clear the area of guards, the person wanting to communicate would whistle "Mary Had a Little Lamb." Everyone would immediately get down on his hands and knees and look through a small crack under his door to insure that his own immediate space was clear of guards. If you saw a Vietnamese in the corridor, you'd cough, the danger signal not to communicate.

Then I spoke. The words poured out of me. I was a traitor. I had answered more questions than name, rank, serial number, and date of birth.

Commander Stockdale heard my brief confession. When I had finished he simply said, "Don't feel like the Lone Ranger." Someone coughed; then all was silent.

The silence lasted throughout the entire day and night that followed. Soon I learned that communication was risky business. We could get off only snatches of conversation in an entire day. The rest of the time we sat alone in our cells. It's hard to describe what solitary confinement can do to unnerve and defeat a man. You quickly tire of standing up or sitting down, sleeping or being awake. There are no books, no paper or pencils, no magazines or newspapers. The only colors you see are drab gray and dirty brown. Months or years may go by when you don't see the sunrise or the moon, green grass or flowers. You are locked in, alone and silent in your filthy little cell breathing stale, rotten air and trying to keep your sanity.

I remembered Edgar Allan Poe's vision of hell in "The Pit and the Pendulum." Poe's hero saw the walls slowly moving toward him, threatening to crush him to death. In Heartbreak Hotel I realized Poe's walls may not have moved at all. It is something in one's head that moves to crush him. I had the best of survival training in the navy, and it got me through that first long day of interrogation. But after that I was alone, and no survival training can prepare a man for years of solitary confinement. What sustains a man in prison is something that he has going for him inside his heart and head—something that happened, or did not happen—back in childhood in the home and church and school. Nobody can teach you to survive the brutality of being alone. At first you panic. You want to cry out. You fight back waves of fear. You want to die, to confess, to do anything to get out of that ever-shrinking world. Then, gradually a plan of defense takes shape. Being alone is another kind of war, but slowly I learned that it, too, can be won. Like a blind man who is forced to develop other senses to replace his useless eyes, a man in solitary confinement must quit regretting what he cannot do and build a new life around what he can do.

Since I couldn't move more than a few feet in any direction, I lay on my bunk and moved my eyes, searching out interesting cracks or scratches in the plaster. Who had made them? What could they mean? Immediately I learned that though no human being shared my tiny space, I was not really alone. The walls were crawling with interesting vermin. Ants fascinated me, and even the rats made entertain-

I literally sprang to that window and pressed my face against the cold iron bars.

ing though ugly roommates. These North Vietnamese rats were unlike any I had ever seen; they were over a foot long and looked like opossums. One old rat was so big I fantasized his stepping out into the corridor and calling, "Here, Kitty, Kitty!" Because I couldn't force myself to eat the bowl of cold seaweed soup with sowbelly fat on the top and could only nibble at the stale French loaf during those first lonely days, my cell was preferred territory to these large, ugly rodents.

More friendly and more agile than the rats were the geckos, six-to-nine-inch-long multicolored lizards with suction cups on their legs. These prehistoric little monsters were wonderful entertainment. They could dart across a wall and snatch an unsuspecting fly or mosquito in mid-flight. I played a game with geckos; lying on my slab, I tried to herd the flies in their direction, celebrating every gecko conquest and keeping score, competing one gecko's accuracy against another.

I developed all kinds of mental games that kept me entertained and edified by the hours. During my short stay at Heartbreak, I also disciplined myself to reconstruct my life, year by year, month by month, day by day. I worked hard to reconstruct and evaluate each event. My memory had rusted over, and I set about scraping the rust away.

In prison I discovered how important regular times of reflection can be. Living in America, one becomes preoccupied with family and career. When I was free, I seldom thought seriously about what I was doing or why I was doing it. When days are filled by travel, conversation, books, papers, movies, television, meals, radio, billboards, and the like, the mind is constantly looking outward and dealing with the world outside and around. But when suddenly all that is taken away, it is forced to deal with the world inside.

At first, this process of remembering was torture; all I

始 no

could think about was food. I thought of Wednesday steak night in the officers' mess on the *Bon Homme Richard:* a six-inch baked potato swimming in butter, sour cream, and chives; hot apple pie with cheese and hot coffee, all I could drink. I though of Mom's chocolate pie or my wife's cooking —anything and everything she put on the table. Then I would see the bowl of rotting pumpkin or seaweed soup and the small loaf of stale French bread in my cell. The thought of swallowing that cold, greasy, repugnant stuff was nauseating. Day by day I refused to eat until my own body fat had been depleted, and my weight began to drop. Soon it became clear that if I didn't eat, I would starve. If I didn't get the necessary protein, I could not survive. Already I was weak and getting weaker.

One day I decided to eat it all. I never really felt full the entire seven years in Vietnam; but every bite of seaweed soup, every small piece of sowbelly fat, every bowl of sewer greens kept me a little closer to health and survival. When one is dying from starvation, a bowl of sewer greens is a gift from God. Before every meal during my captivity, I offered a prayer of thanks. In the past, when others prayed my mind wandered over the day's events or simply waited impatiently for the prayer to end. But in prison, grace was not a routine endured out of habit, guilt, or pressure. To thank God for life seemed the natural thing to do.

During those long periods of enforced reflection, it became so much easier to separate the important from the trivial, the worthwhile from the waste. For example, in the past, I usually worked or played hard on Sundays and had no time for church. For years Phyllis encouraged me to join the family at church. She never nagged or scolded—she just kept hoping. But I was too busy, too preoccupied, to spend one or two short hours a week thinking about the really important things.

Now the sights and sounds and smells of death were all around me. My hunger for spiritual food soon outdid my hunger for a steak. Now I wanted to know about that part of me that will never die. Now I wanted to talk about God and Christ and the church. But in Heartbreak solitary confinement there was no pastor, no Sunday-school teacher, no Bible, no hymnbook, no community of believers to guide and sustain me. I had completely neglected the spiritual dimension of my life. It took prison to show me how empty life is without God, and so I had to go back in my memory to those Sunday-school days in the Nogales Avenue Baptist Church, Tulsa, Oklahoma. If I couldn't have a Bible and hymnbook, I would try to rebuild them in my mind.

I tried desperately to recall snatches of Scripture, sermons, the gospel choruses from childhood, and the hymns we sang in church. The first three dozen songs were relatively easy. Every day I'd try to recall another verse or a new song. One night there was a huge thunderstorm—it was the season of the monsoon rains—and a bolt of lightning knocked out the lights and plunged the entire prison into darkness. I had been going over hymn tunes in my mind and stopped to lie down and sleep when the rains began to fall. The darkened prison echoed with wave after wave of water. Suddenly, I was humming my thirty-seventh song, one I had entirely forgotten since childhood.

> Showers of blessings,
> Showers of blessing we need!
> Mercy drops round us are falling,
> But for the showers we plead.

I no sooner had recalled those words than another song popped into my mind, the theme song of a radio program my mother listened to when I was just a kid.

> Heavenly sunshine, heavenly sunshine
> Flooding my soul with glory divine.
> Heavenly sunshine, heavenly sunshine.
> Hallelujah! Jesus is mine!

Most of my fellow prisoners were struggling like me to rediscover faith, to reconstruct workable value systems. Harry Jenkins lived in a cell nearby during much of my captivity. Often we would use those priceless seconds of communication in a day to help one another recall Scripture verses and stories.

One day I heard him whistle. When the cell block was clear, I waited for his communication, thinking it to be some important news. "I got a new one," he said. "I don't know where it comes from or why I remember it, but it's a story about Ruth and Naomi." He then went on to tell that ancient story of Ruth following Naomi into a hostile new land and finding God's presence and protection there. Harry's urgent news was two thousand years old. It may not seem important to prison life, but we lived off that story for days, rebuilding it, thinking about what it meant, and applying God's ancient words to our predicament.

Everyone knew the Lord's Prayer and the Twenty-Third Psalm, but the camp favorite verse that everyone recalled first and quoted most often is found in the Book of John, third chapter, sixteenth verse.

> For God so loved the world, that he gave his only begotten Son, that whosoever believeth in him should not perish, but have everlasting life.

With Harry's help I even reconstructed the seventeenth and eighteenth verses.

For God sent not his Son into the world to condemn the world; but that the world through him might be saved. He that believeth on him is not condemned: but he that believeth not is condemned already, because he hath not believed in the name of the only begotten Son of God.

How I struggled to recall those Scriptures and hymns! I had spent my first eighteen years in a Southern Baptist Sunday school, and I was amazed at how much I could recall; regrettably, I had not seen then the importance of memorizing verses from the Bible or learning gospel songs. Now, when I needed them, it was too late. I never dreamed that I would spend almost seven years (five of them in solitary confinement) in a prison in North Vietnam or that thinking about one memorized verse could have made a whole day bearable. One portion of a verse I did remember was, "Thy word have I hid in my heart." How often I wished I had really worked to hide God's Word in my heart. I put my mind to work. Every day I planned to accomplish certain tasks. I woke early, did my physical exercises, cleaned up as best I could, then began a period of devotional prayer and meditation. I would pray, hum hymns silently, quote Scripture, and think about what the verses meant to me.

Remember, we weren't playing games. The enemy knew that the best way to break a man's resistance was to crush his spirit in a lonely cell. In other wars, some of our POWs after solitary confinement lay down in a fetal position and died. All this talk of Scripture and hymns may seem boring to some, but it was the way we conquered our enemy and overcame the power of death around us.

It looked as though I would spend my first Christmas in captivity in Heartbreak Hotel; but about 8 P.M. Christmas Eve, 1965, guards entered my cell, blindfolded me, roped me into a jeep with Lt. Commnader Duffy Hutton, and drove us across Hanoi to another prison. It would be my home for two torturously long years.

6

More Torture

Howard Rutledge
The Zoo, Hanoi,
1966 and 1967

To the southwest of downtown Hanoi, there is an old French art colony complete with race track, swimming pool, theater, and assorted living quarters, and service buildings. It must have been quite a showplace at the height of French colonialism. However, by that Christmas Eve, 1965, when I was taken there, some changes had been made.

American prisoners had named this art-colony-turned-prison, the Zoo. Around the place there was a foreboding wall, with guard towers and massive gates. The outbuildings had been stripped of furnishings, the windows had been bricked over, bars covered any opening that remained, individual cells had been constructed in every building, the pool was being used to grow fish for camp officials, the place was overgrown with weeds, and piles of filth were crawling with vermin and rodents. Each building had a name that best indicated the change: the Stable, the Outhouse, and the Pigsty.

Our guards took off our blindfolds and marched me to the Pigsty where I first met the English-speaking interrogator POWs called the Dog. He was large for a Vietnamese and wore a Chinese-type cap with a red star; a cardboard collar-insignia on his olive-drab uniform indicated his rank. I immediately recognized the hated Pigeye standing at his side. It would not belong before I experienced his torture skills again.

The Dog asked me my name and rank. Hoping there might be other Americans present, I shouted out my reply, "Commander Howard Rutledge!" He scribbled on a yellow pad and walked away. Seconds passed.

Then, in the darkness I heard a voice. "Commander Rutledge, come towards the front window." Commander Bill Franke had heard me call out my name. Quickly and quietly he explained where I was. Because it was dark, he couldn't clear the area of guards but promised to communicate the next day.

Cell 4, Pigsty, was approximately 15 x 15 feet. It seemed huge after one month in the closet at Heartbreak. But there was no bed or furnishing, just a cold cement floor. The windows had not yet been bricked in on Cell 4, and the winter cold made my prison feel like an icehouse. Still, I lay back on that cement floor with some hope. After all, I was "on the line"—communicating within thirty seconds of my arrival.

I'll not forget that first Christmas Eve in captivity. It was terribly cold, and though I knew of at least one other American nearby, I was still alone. My body still ached, and my wounds were only beginning to heal. As I lay there in my ice-cold misery, somewhere in my cell a Christmas carol began to play. It was an incredible surprise; I sat up and searched the cell. For a moment I thought my mind was playing treacherous tricks—"Silent Night, Holy Night." The fidelity was awful, but it was the first song I had heard since bailing out more than a month ago. Scratches and all, that carol was beautiful beyond describing.

Then the carol ended, and the voice of Hanoi Hanna came on with a barrage of propaganda. Later I learned that in the walls every cell had a speaker that broadcast bizarre programming for the prisoners. Many of the programs were recorded in the United States and were designed to agitate homesick Americans. "Radio Stateside" may have been a tool to break us down, but the snatches of American music, especially that carol on Christmas Eve, backfired and really boosted my spirits.

I hadn't thought about Christmas carols for my growing list of hymns and gospel songs, but on that strange Christmas Eve, with Hanoi Hanna ranting in the background, I recalled at least eight or ten carols, verse by verse. It was like discovering hidden treasure, and I reveled in it.

On Christmas morning we were awakened early by the camp gong. I hadn't shaved in thirty-two days, and my hair was dirty and extra-long. I was taken to the bathing area and given a haircut and shave. It was primitive but rejuvenating. Americans were not allowed to mix, so the one-by-one trip to the latrine took all of Christmas morning.

Around noon in North Vietnam, the turnkeys (jailers) take a nap. The minimal crew of guards was fairly easy to clear, and in that short hour we could communicate with others without great fear of being caught and punished.

Because I was the new guy at the Zoo, immediately upon clearing the area, everyone wanted to know the latest news from the outside world.

Commander Franke, imprisoned already for five to six months, peered through the crack above his door and whispered the question everyone wanted answered.

"When do you think the war will end?"

Later I learned that across the way listening was Everett Alvarez, the first American POW, downed eighteen months before. How could I tell them it might go on for years? I

36

tried to give them a straightforward message that wouldn't shatter spirits and destroy morale.

"Hang on. We might be here next Christmas."

I could hear the groan pass from cell to cell. Immediately I felt guilty for bringing such bad news, especially at Christmas. Even I never dreamed it would be seven more long years before release.

The next question Bill Franke asked me was, "Do you know the code?"

The first regulation in all the prisons of North Vietnam was DO NOT COMMUNICATE WITH YOUR FELLOW AMERICANS. The enemy knew that if he could isolate a man—make him feel abandoned—cut off—forgotten—he could more easily destroy his resistance and break down his morale. To win this war against our nerves, we had to devise all kinds of ingenious systems to keep the lines open among our fellow prisoners. We learned to think like criminals, to devise ways to lie, cheat, and deceive.

The tap code Commander Franke asked me about was a series of taps and pauses, representing each letter in the alphabet. A man would get down on his hands and knees, wrap himself in a blanket to cut down noise a guard might hear, and tap out messages to the man in an adjoining cell. This man would receive the message, then pass it on to the man next door. Sometimes a message could sweep around the cell block faster than a guard could walk.

"Yes, Bill, I know the code." I had overheard the code being whispered to another prisoner during my short stay at Heartbreak and had memorized it, never realizing I would spend the next seven years using this simple code to tap out messages almost every day.

Communicating was our major weapon against the enemy. Each cell block had a key man who initiated most communication efforts. He usually was located in a place which

37

allowed him the best view of the area. When he gave the signal to clear, each of us would scramble for a position to see if any guards were about. If there were two men in a cell, one would climb on the other's shoulders and look through the high, transom-like windows above the solid wooden doors. Though most of us were kept in solitary confinement, it was advantageous for many reasons to be with another prisoner. You could send messages on the wall, while the other maintained security. Many prisoners in solitary risked punishment daily to send messages and keep the line clear. Often in the midst of communicating, a lone prisoner would be surprised by a guard and severely punished.

Our little tin drinking cups, issued by the enemy, served as effective transducers to get voice or tap messages through solid, cement walls. Every time a new man would enter a prison, his name and rank would be passed quickly to the entire camp and memorized. That way we protected each other. If we knew each other's names, the enemy could not lie or claim they never knew us. I can still reel off more than four hundred names and serial numbers memorized in prison.

That Christmas Day was memorable for more than my first bath and shave. We were fed a turkey dinner. There were many pictures taken by the enemy that day to show how well we were being treated. But perhaps a year went by between those few real meals that we had.

That first New Year's Day of captivity I made at least three resolutions that I repeated each year:

1. I would try never to be cold again.
2. I would try never to be hungry again.
3. I would never be without the Bible again. (This I would put in my mind and my heart.)

38

Our little tin drinking cups, issued by the enemy, served as effective transducers to get voice or tapped messages through solid walls.

Early in January the Dog asked me for a written auto-biographical sketch. Surprisingly, when I refused, he let me go. I was moved from the Pigsty down to a small, solitary cell with no windows where I remained alone until August 1966. Living in a cement box with cement floors, cement walls, and bricked-in windows is like living in a cold-storage vault in the winter and a hotbox in the summer.

Alone in the cell, I continued my devotional periods searching my mind for Scriptures, going over the more than fifty hymns I had recalled. My wrist and leg were almost back to normal. In spite of almost no medical care, my cuts and bruises from the first interrogation had healed. I knew my turn for interrogation would come again. I waited and wondered when.

Early in August the guards came for me. They took me to the "Auditorium," an old theater dressing room, and again the Dog demanded that I write a confession and a biographical sketch. When I refused, they shackled me to the spot and left. A tiny bulb was the only source of light in this spooky torture room. As my eyes became accustomed to the dimness, I could see spiders as big as my fist hanging all around me. They may have been friendly spiders, but they created a terrifying effect in the semidarkness. Ants crawled all over me, and nine million mosquitoes were trapped inside. Gecko lizards scurried through the filth, and large rats looked me over hungarily. It is a helpless sensation to be shackled, hands and feet, in such a place. I had no way to kill the mosquitoes or frighten off the rats. I just sat and watched and trembled.

I sat for four days and nights hardly moving. I remember the third day, August 7, because for two days and nights it had been stifling hot. The third day it rained and those showers of blessings cooled off the cell, and made it almost bearable. Also, August 7 was the day I married Phyllis eighteen years before. Was she well? Did she know I was alive? I missed her so. I breathed a prayer that God would get us through and, if He willed, let me hold her in my arms again.

Each day the Dog or Spot, his assistant, came in to demand a confession, anything in writing the enemy could use against us. I continued to refuse, and on August 8, 1966, the Dog visited me again and insisted once more upon my writing a confession or this time to suffer the punishment of death.

I took the pen, and wrote my choice on the paper, and handed it back to him. DEATH!

They slapped me around and cursed and threatened and demanded something useful in writing.

So I took the pen and wrote again. "I support my country, its government, and its people. I always will." Then I signed it.

August 8, 1966, Pigeye and his friends shackled me, hands and feet, in another torture room, dubbed by those who suffered there, the Outhouse. The Outhouse was located on the south wall of the camp just behind Pigsty. It was a squat, flat-roofed, concrete, bunkerlike room with no windows. The filth in that small room was far beyond anything I had seen to date. In fact, the ants were so plentiful and so large that I am sure by now they've eaten up the entire cement building.

Because it was out in the sun, the temperature inside—and I believe I'm estimating conservatively—was 100 or 110 degrees at midnight.

As I sat there in a pile of human excrement crawling with countless moving things, I thought back upon my "bravery." It was not bravery to ask for death when the enemy needed us alive, but I knew the cost I would pay for my resistance. Again it took all the courage I could muster. Now I sat staring into the darkness, gagging on the odor, my skin crawling with pests that bit and pinched in the dark. My courage waned. Maybe they wouldn't kill me. Maybe they would just abuse me until I died.

I remained in the Outhouse, my hands cuffed behind my back, my legs in irons. They gave me only a small bowl of rice each day and two cups of filthy water. It was unbearably hot, and by the end of the first week I was very sick with dysentery and couldn't eat. For almost three weeks I sat getting weaker each day from the constant diarrhea and the lack of food and water. There was a bucket in the room in which to perform the bodily functions, but it is difficult when you're handcuffed with your arms behind your back and your legs in irons, and you're too weak to move. So I and the prisoners before me just relieved ourselves in our clothing and on the floor. No one ever cleaned the Outhouse. To keep us lying in that filth was part of the plan.

By the third week I had developed a heat rash that itched and bled, and left me feeling close to despair. Our camp policy was to hold on until just short of losing touch with reality and then volunteer to confess in writing. While we still had some senses left, we could usually write a confession anyone but our enemy could tell was false. I decided that if each of us could take thirty days in that torture room in one year, only twelve would suffer, and some men might even be spared.

Each night was getting harder and harder to endure. I would work my mind furiously in the daytime, hoping to be tired enough at night to sleep in spite of heat rash, dysentery, hunger, and pain. All day I planned to get through just one more night and then confess, but in the morning I would feel new strength to bear one more day and night.

On August 31, after twenty-eight days of torture, I could remember I had children but not how many. I said Phyllis's name over and over again so I would not forget. I prayed

42

for strength. It was on that twenty-eighth night I made God a promise. If I survived this ordeal, the first Sunday back in freedom I would take Phyllis and my family to their church and at the close of the service confess my faith in Christ and join the church. This wasn't a deal with God to get me through that last miserable night. It was a promise made after months of thought. It took prison and hours of painful reflection to realize how much I needed God and the community of believers. After I made God that promise, again I prayed for strength to make it through the night.

When the morning dawned through the crack in the bottom of that solid prison door, I thanked God for His mercy and called the guard.

Immediately upon hearing my willingness to write, the guards released me, I was taken to a bath and cleaned, then taken to the Fox, the commander of the Zoo, to sign my "confession."

"I am a Yankee imperialist aggressor," I wrote, parroting their text, knowing how little those words sounded like anything an American would write. I knew they had not released my name yet after nine months and that confession could be used against me to humiliate me in the camp and as propaganda around the world. I hoped my friends and family would understand.

Every POW had his breaking point. Some of us have lasted longer than others, but each of us eventually gave in, in order to survive. To point out the men who broke early in the game, to draw charges or make accusations now, would be to underestimate the enemy's skill and the power of fear and loneliness and pain.

7

More Grief

Phyllis Rutledge
San Diego, California,
1966 & 1967

The children were growing up fast, and I had to be both mom and dad to all of them. Sondra was a teen-ager with boyfriends and dates to think about. Helping her through those awkward teen-age years was an awesome responsibility. I've always been too easygoing. Howard had always disciplined the children. He made the rules. He enforced them. Now with Howard gone, it was my task to get my daughters through. Fortunately, I had been a teen-age girl once and had some experience to fall back on.

Raising John was something else. He was a wonderful boy, and like his father he was full of energy and strong-willed. He was often in trouble for his temper. John was lonely and angry. He missed his father very much and needed a man in his life.

I knew how he felt. I needed a man in my life, too. But Howard was not dead. He was missing. So, I was not a wife I was not a widow. I was nothing. I still loved Howard and never thought once of ending our marriage. So John, Sondra, the little girls, and their unhappy mother would just have to wait and see what happened next.

I got really despondent during those first two years. I would pray and pray and nothing would happen. Often I would ask God, "Just let me have anything to know that Howard is alive and that all of this suffering is good for something." It seemed my prayers went unanswered.

There were some little answers we clung to along the way, hoping that God had heard our prayers. For example, my mother-in-law received an envelope with a foreign tea bag inside. It was addressed to Howard's dad who had passed away just before Howard had been shot down. We wondered if someone was trying to send us a message. I knew if Howard were trying to communicate in code, it might possibly be from the Bible. So, scratching at straws, I looked up *tea* in our Bible concordance. I found one Scripture in the Book of Haggai. The verse included such lines as "I have just enough to eat to keep from being hungry. I have just enough clothing to keep from being cold." That fit our idea of prison perfectly so our hopes soared. Then I realized that Howard hadn't read the Bible in years. Surely he wouldn't begin using it with a passage from an obscure Old Testament book like Haggai!

Finally, we sent the bag to navy authorities who reported back that some crackpot was sending them around indiscriminately to other families.

I was really desperate. It seemed that God had abandoned us. Our church attendance and our spirits fell.

Howard and I were both reared in loyal Southern Baptist households. In our homes, as children, it was family tradition to attend church every time the church doors opened. We would go to Sunday school faithfully and stay for morning worship. Sunday nights the family would all go back for choir practice and Baptist Training Union. On Wednesday nights we went to Bible study and prayer meeting, while Thursday nights we often joined the evangelism visitation teams of our church.

But something happened when Howard and I got married. Stationed at Pensacola, Howard only went to church three or four times and then dropped out completely. Every time I asked him to join us at church, he would answer, "Not today, Honey. I'm too tired," or "I think I'll just stay at home and read the paper," or "There's a ball game on TV, and it's my only chance to relax and see one."

He was never sarcastic, nor did he try to get me to stop going. He just lost interest himself. Howard's career was really climbing. He said he couldn't be active in church the way he should be and still be a good fighter pilot. He got active in the happy-hour cocktail circuit on Friday nights and eventually threw off all the constraints his parents had enforced during those teen-age years.

We never had liquor in our homes as children. We never went to shows on Sundays, never even played cards, and any kind of swearing was rewarded with a mouthful of soap or a switching. Now, Howard was boss in his own family, and he rebelled against his strict Oklahoma Baptist background.

By the time we had children, the only services Howard would attend were the memorial services for his friends lost in battle.

For a while, in Jacksonville, I had a friend whose pilot husband also was losing interest in the church. We would plot and scheme to get our husbands there. Every Sunday morning I would look around the congregation to see if she had her husband in tow. She would give the A-OK sign if her husband was there or look discouraged and shake her head if he wasn't. It was kind of comical at first. Eventually, we both quit trying.

I was worried what his not attending church would do to our children. When Sundays came around and I went through the house saying, "Get up, it's time for Sunday school," I was answered by a series of groans. "Daddy's not going; why should we go?" After Howard disappeared, I grew more and more depressed. Feeling pity for myself, it was easier just to stay in bed on Sundays. Eventually I dropped out of church, too.

One afternoon two years after Howard was shot down, I was visiting my mother when she became very ill. She had had a stroke; and only days after the operation to save her, she died. During her funeral I cried tears of guilt for all those things I should have done. I should have written more; I should have called more. I loved my mother, but in my preoccupation with survival, I had seldom even seen her in the past few years. Now I felt guilty and even more alone. First Howard is shot down—now this! What tragedy would strike us next?

8

My First Roommate

*Howard Rutledge
Las Vegas, Hanoi,
January-October, 1967*

I left the Zoo with nineteen other men and traveled back
across Hanoi to the Hanoi Hilton. The enemy had opened
a new section, promptly dubbed *Las Vegas* by the prisoners,
in the immense Hoa Lo prison complex. Six cell blocks
ringed a courtyard area. On the north wall was the Thunder-
bird. On the Northeast corner was the Mint. Then came the
Desert Inn and the Stardust along the east wall. The Riviera,
on the south wall, and the Golden Nugget on the west completed the square.

In the courtyard were ten small bathing areas appropri-
ately named the Sands. You can imagine what kind of baths
they were. In fact, by May there was no water at all to fill
the basins, so the enemy dug three wells in the Las Vegas
courtyard. Because there was no sewer system, everything
was dumped in holes beside the wells; therefore, the water
we dipped to wash our clothes and to bathe was ultimately
sewage, filthy with fungus and crawling with worms.

Inside each cell block was an assortment of cells ranging
from 4-man units in a 9 x 9 foot space, to 2-men units in a
4 x 8 foot space, and in the Mint the smallest cells I had

even seen—total space 3 feet wide and just over 6 feet long. A hardwood bed on one wall left less than 1 x 6 foot space to walk and exercise in. At the foot of every bed in Las Vegas was a set of stocks to shackle an offending prisoner to his slab.

Apparently the enemy knew how effective our communication systems had become and had built Las Vegas to cut down our wall-tap system. They left a two-foot dead space between the cells so that prisoners could no longer share a common wall. We just continued tapping on the floor or common perimeter wall, and all their extra work didn't ever slow us down. We continued to communicate, to organize, and resist.

By now communication among the prisoners had become immensely effective. The enemy needed prisoner cooperation to make its propaganda tapes and to meet its press and protest delegations. The easiest victim was the new guy freshly captured who walked innocently into the enemy's trap. However, no sooner had the new guy entered the Hanoi Hilton than the prisoner-communication network got to him, briefed him on in-camp resistance policy, and turned him almost overnight into a seasoned resister.

During those long years of captivity, we learned to communicate with anything and everything. Under ideal circumstances—which seldom came—we could grab off a few minutes of face-to-face communications. As I explained earlier, we used tin cups as transducers to tap or talk coded messages through solid walls. For short distances we tapped with fingers; for longer distances we tapped with the ball of fist or elbows against the floor. Other legitimate noises were never wasted—a cough, a sniff, spitting, and/or clearing the throat were converted into simple communication efforts. One specially effective ruse was to sweep through a compound, using the broom movement to signal messages to the entire area. Or, if a man walked by another's cell, he could drag his little Ho-Chi-Minh sandals in code. When he cleaned out his "honey bucket," he swept and cleaned it with a bamboo broom. Often with the guards looking on, men pounded out messages on those pails with the enemy none the wiser.

We began to think like criminals. I have spent as much as ten hours a day staring at a two-inch drain hole trying to track and clear a guard so that I could grab five minutes of conversation on the wall. Tracking a guard revealed his habits, identified his routines. In two-man cells one prisoner sat on another's shoulder watching the guard, memorizing every regular move he made. When we had visual sightings of each other, we communicated with semaphore code or hand flash movements like the deaf use. If someone could see under the door opposite (through the crack), he could tap out messages with his toe to the prisoner across the corridor.

We even wrote coded messages to each other, using any scrap paper, including toilet paper, and writing with ink made of cigarette ashes or blood and water. We would take a piece of wire from a screen or a stick from the floor, tear off the bottom of old lead toothpaste rolls, and make a pencil. Charcoal and lye soap mixed together in the right proportions make an excellent crayon.

The enemy realized our communications system was beating them. We were isolated into small cells, yet the whole camp was organized and informed. I often fantasized about how I would enjoy taking a high North Vietnamese visitor through all the cell blocks, pointing out the name, rank, serial number, place of birth, date of capture, and even the favorite Scripture or food of every man in every cell block, even those areas I had never visited because through covert communications we could know almost that

We were shackled in our leg irons, handcuffed behind our
backs in this position day and night.

much about the camp.

However, our successes led eventually to painful reprisal. The enemy began a vicious crackdown, punishing men caught in the act of communicating with swift and unforgettable vengeance. There were small portholes in the cell doors; a guard could flip that door and catch a man without warning. Little child-size handcuffs would force the elbows together painfully, and we would be left in them for weeks at a time; or we were shackled in leg irons, handcuffed behind our backs, and left on our beds in this position day and night.

Later on, this cruelty was compounded by blindfolding a prisoner. If he cried out, he would be gagged with a rag. Also there were the little milking stools the prisoners sat on during interrogation. An offender would be forced to sit on the stool as long as he could, seven, maybe ten days. Of course, without sleep or rest, hallucinations start. If the offender moved, the guard would beat him. It was very severe punishment.

April 24, 1967, after only four months in Las Vegas, I was called to interrogation by an English-speaking officer we had dubbed the Rat. He surprised me with the news that after 540 days of solitary confinement I would have a roommate. That day I moved into Cell 6 of the Desert Inn, with Air Force Captain George McKnight, whom I had covertly talked with back in Heartbreak an eternity ago. Both of us were incorrigible. He had been at another camp near Hanoi, nicknamed the Briarpatch, and had suffered treatment similar to my own. Like my twenty-eight days in the Outhouse and the Auditorium, George had spent thirty-four days, hands cuffed behind his back, in a hole in the ground before he finally gave up and wrote his "confession."

For eighteen months I had experienced only snatches of covert conversation with anyone. He, too, had suffered under silence. The result was hilarious. We talked nonstop for three days and nights. In seventy-two hours of conversation, you can learn a lot about a man. One of the first things I asked him was, "George, do you know any Scripture?"

There was a long pause, and for a moment I thought I had landed a roommate totally uninterested in such things. Then slowly he replied, "No, I don't! I'm sorry." So during those next days together he listened to mine.

George is a bachelor. Apparently he was quite a swinger and called himself Peck's Bad Boy. But in prison he, too, had thought a lot about Christ and his church. He was a Catholic and had tied knots in a string to create a makeshift rosary. Every morning he would pray using the rosary, pacing in the little walk space we had. I would sit on the bed for my devotional.

Perhaps before I was shot down I had some prejudices against Catholics based on childhood misconceptions. I remembered talk of purgatory and limbo and the pope. But locked together in a tiny cell in a North Vietnamese prison, it didn't take the two of us long to get past such things that separated us to the common faith we felt in Christ.

Don't misunderstand. We weren't two fully-developed saints sitting dispassionately through the day discussing theology. There probably wasn't a thimbleful of serious theology between us. We just knew that without our faith in God, without our common belief that He was with us, we could not have made it through.

Prison life was rough. We were treated like animals, so, I am afraid, we developed some rather crude behavior in the process. One example was our constant use of four-letter words. Even covert communications were sometimes sprinkled with rough language. George and I both were quick-tempered and took pleasure in throwing out a curse to a guard. Because he couldn't understand English, we could smile and tell him in no uncertain terms how we felt about his brutality, and he had no idea how thoroughly he had been insulted. Swearing was one of the few pleasures we had. Nevertheless, we both knew that profanity was a crutch and a bad habit that needed breaking.

One day George and I made a pact. We would start on Sunday and go seven days; we would each keep track of the other's swear words, numbering them, and the person with the fewest slips would receive a precious banana at the end of the week. We may have had to steal the banana from a careless guard, but we weren't working on a cure for stealing that week!

After I had spent a year and a half alone, George Mc-Knight, a Catholic brother-in-Christ, brought me new strength to face the years of prison that lay ahead. If I can help it, I will never try again to "go it alone." Those wild, hilarious, stimulating, prayerful nights of sharing we spent together in Las Vegas made me realize how much we need each other. The experience renewed my resolution made in the Outhouse, to join my family's church as one of my first acts upon reaching freedom and to take again my responsible place in Christ's body on earth.

On May 19 I was called before the senior interrogator at Las Vegas and asked to say something nice about prison treatment. I told him simply and clearly that the year and a half that Captain McKnight and I had spent in solitary confinement was the severest form of mental cruelty. Needless to say, he didn't take kindly to my remarks.

I'll not forget that night. Tensions were high. The heat had been miserable and our communications system was ruining the enemy's plans to use us in its propaganda war. The lights blinked on and off. Apparently the interrogator was a chain smoker, and cigarette rations were down, so he was trying in the semidarkness to roll his own. Suddenly our bombers struck Hanoi with unusual fury. The sirens sounded wildly, and the bombs began to fall around us, splitting the silence and rocking nearby targets. He exploded into a rage. I knew my days of living with the luxury of a roommate had ended. Two days later the guards entered my cell and took me to one of those 3 x 6 cells in the Mint. The pressure was on again.

The Mint was a filthy place. The enemy had built a pig-pen in the alley around the cells to house the camp's pigs. The smell of those pigs slopping through the filth outside my window, together with the din of squealing that they made, was quite a change from the long nights of quiet conversation with George.

But being alone again was even more of a shock. I knew that (for my sanity's sake) I had to reestablish my system of discipline immediately. By May of 1967 I had developed over one hundred hymns and Scriptures by memory. Of course, they weren't perfect; in fact, back in freedom now I'm having to check them out and rememorize them correctly. But they were mine, and I had a regular program each day in my cell to go over them one by one.

My routine included rising early and charting my day. The key was to plan more tasks than I could possibly accomplish. I spent the morning pacing the cell in three steps, then turning around and pacing back again—back and forth every morning, humming quietly every hymn I knew, repeating the words, verse by verse in my mind. I had arranged the songs in groups of five. I would wind up each group with a prayer, first for my daughters Peggy and Barbara, then another group of five hymns and prayers for my oldest daughter Sondra, then five more hymns for my son John, then five more for my wife Phyllis, and then my mother, and so forth. I would quote through my Scriptures or pick a word and try to develop that word into another hymn or

Scripture buried deep in my memory, waiting to be discovered.

One day I thought of the word cymbal and the phrase
"sounding brass and tinkling cymbal," fell into place. Eventually I reconstructed that whole love poem in 1 Corinthians
13, but the Apostle Paul would have looked with horror at
my arrangement of his masterpiece. I began with "Now
abideth faith, hope and love, but the greatest of these is
love," and went backwards from there through a dozen or
so verses, ending with "sounding brass and tinkling cymbal."
I had the whole thing totally out of order; the first verse was
the last; the last, first. So, I messed up, but the thoughts were
right, and often those verses sustained me.

My system was a mind-saver; but after twenty-seven days
of conversation with another human being, I had to get "on
the line" again. I guess I was out of practice and tapped out
a message to a cell nearby before the area had been thoroughly cleared. A guard surprised me in the act, and I was
punished.

He shackled me to my slab in rear cuffs and irons. For
five days I couldn't move. It was summer and very hot. The
humidity must have been in the 90s, the temperature in the
100s. I developed one of those severe heat rashes where the
red welts turn to blisters and ultimately to boils. At first I
wasn't too concerned about the boils. But they wouldn't
come to a head, so I'd have to pick them to stop the swelling.
I didn't know the pus was contagious or that the bug inside
the poison caused the boils to spread. In a few days I
counted at least sixty boils about one inch in diameter over
my entire body—under my arms, in my nose, in my hair,
on my ears, legs, hands, and fingers.

I couldn't bathe. The water itself was crawling with filth
to infect the open sores. I tried putting lye soap on the boils,
but that only seemed to irritate them more.

My First Roommate

Finally the boils got so bad I felt like Job. They began to attack my spirit. I prayed often through those miserable nights for God to heal them. I don't know why God answers some prayers with relief and others with silence. But like Job I could only go on trusting Him. The alternatives are too bleak to consider. It wasn't long until I received my second act of kindness from the enemy; a medic gave me some sulfa pills, and in a few days the boils were gone.

9

The Alcatraz Gang

Howard Rutledge
Alcatraz, Hanoi,
1968 and 1969

In the absolute center of Hanoi, right behind the National Ministry of Defense, is a walled, island-like prison called Alcatraz. No more than 50 x 50 feet in size, this maximal security area contains only two buildings—one housing three cells; the other housing ten. Alcatraz had been a high security prison built by the French for their VIP prisoners.

On October 25, 1967, eleven of us with reputations as POW incorrigibles were chosen by the enemy to be transported immediately to Alcatraz. We were, for the most part, senior officers who had taken active resistance roles, establishing communications and encouraging noncooperation. The North Vietnamese isolated us in the heart of their capital to put us out of circulation and to help curtail the resistance movement. We promptly nicknamed ourselves "The Alcatraz Gang."

There was Commander Jim Stockdale from Illinois, the senior ranking naval officer whose policies in Las Vegas during the summer of '67 had been so effective; and Commander Jerry Denton from Mobile, Alabama, second senior naval officer whose great leadership organized the Zoo in

'66. Both men were active communicators and aggressive leaders. Commander Harry Jenkins, Washington, D.C.; Capt. Jim Mulligan, Lawrence, Massachusetts; and I were also senior naval officers and each had resistance as reasons for our sentence.

Air Force Captain Ron Storz was there, another effective communicator from New York, who administered Jim Stockdale's policies in Las Vegas, as was Comdr. Bob Shumaker, second pilot captured in 1965, a resister who gave the enemy nothing but trouble. Then there was Air Force Capt. George McKnight, my old roommate, and Navy Lt. George Coker. Both earned their ticket for having escaped from Dirty Bird prison in October '67. Upon recapture they were singled out for the honor of joining us at Alcatraz.

The last two men were Major Sam Johnson from Texas, a hard resister, and Lt. Commander Nels Tanner, a navy man from Tennessee. Nels had earned his ticket to Alcatraz in a press conference in Hanoi where he "confessed" with a straight face and sincere voice that there were at least two turncoat pilots in his squadron. They were Ben Casey and Clark Kent! Of course television audiences around the world immediately recognized Doctor Casey and Superman from a popular TV show and comic-page fame and laughed that propaganda bulletin to shame.

But there was nothing funny about Alcatraz. Each cell had a cement sleeping slab and a walking area no more than four feet square. There were no windows, and the small transom-like space above the solid iron door had been very neatly secured with a steel plate. At last we knew the truth about the old refrigerator joke—when the guards closed the door, the light really did go out. In the winter the cells were refrigerator cold, and in the summer they were stifling.

To make matters worse, we spent fifteen hours a day with our legs in shackles. Every night we slept in those 10-

to 20-pound leg irons. In the winter they got icy-cold beneath our thin blankets, and in summer they cooked us. We were unshackled on the Tet holiday and at Christmas, but for sixteen months we wore them almost every day.

Immediately, in spite of the handicaps, we set up a communication system. Through covert communication techniques—tapping, semaphore, quick snatches of conversation, coded notes, coughs, sneezes, and the tapping broom or sliding Ho-Chi-Minh sandals—we talked to each other every day. Soon we were sharing intimate details about each other's family life, military career, and religious faith. There may have been cement and iron walls separating each man from the next, but by now we had all learned how important each man was to the other. Our circle of friendship grew strong and intimate. I thik I can honestly say, the more we knew about each man's strengths or weaknesses, the more we loved each other.

The Vietnamese tried to exploit us one against the other. They tried to get us to contribute propaganda statements or tapes, and when we refused, we were punished. The interrogation room was also used for torture; and when one of us went inside we all suffered with him. We had no secrets, and the bonds of friendship built there will last an eternity.

By now, most of us had suffered from torture and deprivation. We received almost no medicine during our entire prison terms, and because our two daily meals consisted primarily of pumpkin or cabbage soup with a few pieces of pig fat floating on the greasy surface, our protein intake was extremely low. Therefore, our resistance to disease and infection was down; we had to be extremely careful. If we stubbed a toe, we knew we would lose a toenail. Because we received little, if any, medical assistance during those long years of prison, we had to devise home remedies.

For the ever-present diarrhea, dysentery, or flu, pieces of charcoal salvaged from a dump pile might help. For skin infections or serious cuts and scratches, we washed with lye soap and bore the irritation to achieve healing. Our intestines were crawling with worms that would work their way out through our system in surprising ways. One night Harry woke up with what he thought was a piece of string in his mouth. He pulled out a six-inch worm! Now and then the enemy would throw a red pepper into our soup. We soon discovered that the pepper cleaned out worms. When no peppers were available, we tried to steal a drink of kerosene from a lantern. That quick snort of stolen kerosene fixed the worms and almost fixed the thief who had them.

We did what we could to keep each other's spirits high. One favorite method was to sweep out messages of encouragement to the entire compound with our broom. Each morning one by one we would dump our bucket in the hole near the latrine. Jerry Denton would be the last man down, and he would sweep out the latrine area, slowly using each stroke to communicate in code.

One day in 1968 we were all believing the war must end soon; the bombing had increased, and we were looking for a sign of hope. Day by day we waited, and day by day no sign came. The morale was down when Jerry went to clean that day. We listened as he tapped, "In Thy gentle hands, we are smiling our thanks!" It was a strange message but an important reminder that in spite of our hopelessness, we could be thankful. Jerry helped me remember my blessings, though small, for gratitude was the way to defeat the power of loneliness and fear. I found, even in Alcatraz, plenty to be thankful for, and it made all the difference.

During those days I worked my mind double time to stave off the temptation to lie down and die. I built five houses in my imagination during my seven years in North Vietnam.

Carefully I selected the site, then negotiated with its owner for purchase. Personally, I cleared the ground, dug the foundations, laid the cement, put up the walls, shingled the roof, and landscaped the property. After I had carefully furnished the home, I sold it, took my profit, and began the entire process once again. I'll probably never build my own home in freedom, but in solitary confinement I enjoyed the mental exercise, nail by nail, and can recall today each stage of every house I built.

I also reconstructed, day by day, my childhood in Tulsa, my marriage to Phyllis, and the growth of our family. I soon realized how insensitive I had been with my family and how preoccupied I had become with my own interests. I had dropped out of church almost immediately after marriage and left my family to develop their spiritual life on their own. One memory that especially haunted me was a trip to El Paso that I made with Phyllis and the children. I was feeling guilty for paying them so little attention, and so to compensate, I offered them money to buy any Mexican merchandise they desired. I showed John the beautiful leather goods, the elaborate stone chess sets, and the colorful peasant shirts and sandals. He chose a rather amateurish sketch of Jesus in a rough wooden frame. I had offered him anything, and when he chose that rather ugly picture, I plainly showed my disappointment. Every time in prison I recalled my thoughtless insensitive reaction, I got a knot in my stomach.

Here my young son was already showing interest in something more than baseball and routine chores. He was sending me signals loud and clear, and I missed them. How many signals I must have missed from Phyllis, Sondra, Peggy, Barbara, as well as John. I was too busy doing "other things" to really be a dad. How I regretted those late-night cocktail parties that seemed strategic to my life. I decided

I remember Alcatraz as a time of loneliness and misery,
constant harassment, torture, and interrogation.

in Vietnam that if I were ever free again, I would try to listen, try to understand, and try to show spiritual leadership in my home and with my family.

Every day in Alcatraz I repeated my devotional routine, my prayers, Scripture quoting, and my songs. By now I could quote about 120 hymns and Scriptures. But every day it got harder to believe we would ever really be free again. It seemed the war would never end. I remember Alcatraz as a time of loneliness and misery, constant harassment, torture, and interrogation; but I don't remember one of the Alcatraz Gang ever losing faith in God or in his country.

Alcatraz is the source of my saddest memory of all my POW experiences. Eleven of us went in. Only ten came back. Ron Storz, the sensitive, young, air force captain from New York, was not really well upon arrival at Alcatraz; but in spite of physical weakness, he was a real leader. His message by example was "unity over self." An able, aggressive communicator, Ron loved to tap out messages with the broom. He was an Episcopalian and a sensitive Christian brother. One day in 1969 he swept through that compound a message that was perhaps the most effective sermon I have ever heard. "Seek God here! This is where you'll find Him."

Like all of us he was probably wrestling with his increasing anxiety to get out of that miserable place and into the light again. But when freedom didn't come, he reminded us all plainly to quit sulking and get down to the important business of seeking God now, rather than waiting for some better time or place.

One day Ron swept a very different kind of message. With his broom he tapped, "God, hear my cries." We all knew Ron was very ill. He was getting weaker and his weight had dropped from around 175 pounds to just over 100. He was quite emaciated, and even the enemy was growing aware of his plight. One day Frenchy, our interrogator, approached

Ron in our corridor and told him he would have to move to the larger interrogation room and out of the tiny cell.

Ron argued loudly to stay with his friends. All he wanted was a roommate. After months of solitary confinement, he needed to talk to someone. The enemy had permitted Ron no letters from home and now even though they knew his mental and physical strengths were depreciating rapidly they would not give him a roommate. They tried to separate Ron from the rest of us, but Ron would not go.

Finally, Frenchy had to explain that in a few short hours his friends would be leaving Alcatraz and that he would have to remain. The Vietnamese were not hard on Ron that night. They did not make him move. All of us had heard it. Frenchy said tonight we would be moving out. After almost two years in Alcatraz, we would be leaving. That night we moved, one at a time, into a waiting truck, past Ron in his lonely cell. It was one of the hardest moments of my life as a POW. The worst part of being a prisoner is the helplessness to reach out and lift up another man in need. We couldn't even say good-by. They had the burp guns. They had the power.

War is like that for both sides. I'm sure the enemy had families who bled and died. I'm sure the enemy cried when loved ones went away and did not return. I'm sure they, too, were tempted to give way to anger and hatred. But revenge is God's business. Anger and hatred can destroy us all. When it's over, we must try to forget and to forgive.

We never stopped praying for Ron and for his family, but we knew we would probably never see him again until that day God chose to reunite the Alcatraz Gang in another world free from such pain and sorrow.

Another Tragedy

10

Phyllis Rutledge
San Diego, California,
July 4, 1968

There is an old superstition that bad news comes in a series of three happenings. In 1965 I "lost" Howard; in 1967 I lost Mother.

The third tragic blow fell on July 4, 1968. School was out. The children were restless. The house was full of John's and Sondra's teen-age friends. I had planned on sending John to Oklahoma to spend the summer with my sister and her son, but she beat me to the punch and sent her boy to spend the summer with me. We planned a July 4 picnic at the beach. The summer before, at a similar picnic in Tulsa, my sister had been injured in the head by a firework tossed from a crowd, so we tried to find a quiet beach away from holiday dangers.

John was like a fish in the ocean. He and his visiting cousin, Mark, loved to see which one could hold his breath the longest under water. They were diving and swimming and having a great time. On one particular dive John stayed under far too long. Suddenly, I could see a black boy pulling a white boy through the surf, one arm around his waist and the other around his neck. It was John, and it looked as if

66

he had drowned. I ran to his side in panic. Apparently, he had dived into the water and struck his head on a rock beneath the surface. The stranger saved my boy from drowning. I never even had the opportunity to thank him.

We called an ambulance and rushed John to the emergency hospital. The first person I thought to call was Pastor Foley. He came immediately. An outstanding young neurosurgeon happened to be on the staff of that hospital and recommended immediate surgery. Brother Foley had been a medic in World War II. He explained the options and after he prayed, I decided to permit the operation. Then we waited. During those endless hours, I prayed. It was the first time I had prayed in months, but I prayed hard. "Don't let John die!" It seemed the past few years I had had to watch all my family suffer. I felt so helpless. I wanted to bear their pain, but all that I could do was stand helplessly by.

Finally, the surgeons walked out of the operating room and sat down beside me. I could tell their news was bad news.

"Mrs. Rutledge, your son is paralyzed from the neck down. He is alive but will probably never move again."

John was only fifteen years old. He was just becoming a man. He had so much life ahead of him, and now he was paralyzed. How much grief were we to bear? Where was God in all this? Was he punishing us for something I had or hadn't done? Was He testing me?

Brother Foley talked softly of a God who stood helplessly by as His own Son, Jesus, died on a Roman cross. With tears in his eyes, Pastor Foley talked about a heavenly Father who understood our pain and shared our sorrow. We can't understand the mystery of suffering. But we can know that God has promised never to leave us or forsake us. The words poured out, and somehow I got hold of hope. I didn't understand the tragedy that struck my son that day. I felt guilty and responsible, but I prayed for strength, and God heard my prayer.

11

New Hope

*Howard Rutledge
Hanoi, Hilton,
1970*

As the enemy's trucks carted us away from Alcatraz that cold, winter night in December 1969 we dared to hope that the nightmare was ending and that we were going home. But when the blindfolds were removed and we were standing once again beneath the walls of the Hanoi Hilton, our hope died. The guards escorted us past New Guy Village and Heartbreak Hotel, and the iron doors of Las Vegas swung open to receive us once again.

Everything seemed the same. The place was as bleak and cold and filthy as ever. The waters of the Sands still ran thick with sewage, alive with parasites of every description. Men were still crowded into cells not big enough for animals, and the pigs still slopped in troughs around the Mint, my wretched home in '67.

I felt agony and anger as the turnkey slammed that iron door and I found myself once again in solitary confinement. This time my home was a cramped cell in Cell Block Stardust. It was like repeating a bad dream. Would it all begin again, the long interrogations, the threats, the torture? Had nothing changed?

Little by little it dawned that something had changed at Las Vegas. There were no agonizing cries in the night from torture rooms. There were no fresh rope burns, no new broken bones. Physical torture had ended, or so it seemed. The rumor spread. Hope mounted.

Soon the Cat himself confirmed our suspicions. Major Bai, chief North Vietnamese staff officer and supervisor of the various prison-camp commanders throughout Hanoi, told Jerry Denton and me that prisoners would no longer suffer physical torture and abuse. Speaking quietly and in broken English, his former cocky manner subdued, his spirit broken, the Cat explained the reason.

"I have misinterpreted the will of the Vietnamese people," he told us. "For four thousand years the policy of the people has been humane and lenient treatment toward prisoners. I have misread and misinterpreted the party's will. I have gone before the people and confessed." Soon after his strange confession, Major Bai disappeared from the Hoa Lo prison complex, and, to my knowledge, he has not been seen again.

Was the Cat speaking truth? Would the torture end? Why had the policy been changed? With growing excitement, the questions raced though our minds. We didn't know about the volunteer organizations in America that were working so hard through bracelets and bumper stickers to keep our plight before the public. We hadn't heard about the strenuous efforts on our behalf by the world's leaders, the International Red Cross, and patriotic organizations all across our country. We couldn't know about the thousands of letters and cables the North Vietnamese were receiving from the little people all around the world. We only knew that the Cat had spoken to a few of us, and the word needed to be spread.

However, most senior officers were still living in solitary

I followed last, lagging behind just long enough to whisper the
code.

confinement, and it would be no small task to get such news spread quickly and convincingly from our cell block to other cell blocks within the Hanoi Hilton and throughout Hanoi to the other prisons: the Plantation, the Son Tay Camps Faith and Hope, and the Zoo. But to get the word out was imperative, because the enemy was still using threats of torture and coercion to get us to submit and to cooperate in its propaganda campaign.

Alan Paton once wrote in his *Cry the Beloved Country* that men are held "by chains of fear and fear of chains." We had to put the prisoners' minds at rest. We didn't need to fear. Resistance would not be met with torture. Fortunately, the Alcatraz Gang had gone to work immediately to establish lines of communication, and it wasn't long until the word was out.

The Asian flu was spreading through Hanoi about this time, and at least 75 to 80 percent of the prisoners in the camp came down with high fever and dysentery. For three days I couldn't move off my plank bed. Then, just as I was getting strong enough to sit up and stare another bowl of rotten-cabbage soup in the face, a guard opened my door, and in walked Harry Jenkins. It was Wednesday night, February 25, 1970, and during more than four years of captivity, I had lived outside of solitary confinement for only twenty-seven wonderful days with George McKnight. During all my years in prison, I had not been more than thirty feet away from Commander Jenkins, and we knew each other intimately through our covert communication efforts. But after four years, to shake his hand and know that when the turn-key walked away, I would be face-to-face with another human being—and not alone—was something else!

We talked nonstop for several days and nights. It may have been in whispers, but the sound of our voices was like music. Sometimes we would go for years without using our voices in prison. Several times I honestly was afraid that when I tried to speak again, nothing would happen. But during those next thirty days with Jenkins it happened around the clock. Even with the thousands of words we got off during those first days, few were wasted. Fighting doesn't end because a man's plane is shot down or his squad is captured. The war isn't over for a man thrown into a high security, escape-proof prison. The prisoner of war works round the clock to beat the enemy, and Harry and I had much to accomplish in the short time we had together.

A prisoner in the Desert Inn cell block in Las Vegas was having trouble getting "on the line." He didn't know the code and needed tutoring; this was our chance to teach him letter by letter how to communicate. Fortunately Waldo, one of our regular camp guards, was not too bright. With Waldo's help we could get the new man "on the line" and mend the broken communications link.

The plan was simple. On our daily walks to the latrine dumping area, Harry would try walking so close to Waldo that the poor, unsuspecting guard would never see me lagging back just long enough to whisper the code, bit by bit, to the new man in Desert Inn.

It worked! The sight must have caused a lot of stifled laughter to any prisoner who might have been watching this charade through transom slit or barred window. First came Waldo, shuffling along, mumbling to himself. Then Harry followed, literally tripping over Waldo's heels, clicking our honey pots together now and then, and making sufficient heavy breathing and noisy footsteps for the two of us. I followed last, lagging behind just long enough to whisper the code, then running madly to catch up before Waldo got the wiser. He never suspected a thing, and in a matter of days the new man was "on the line."

We assigned ourselves, or were assigned, important tasks

to accomplish every day. Surveillance of the camp area became an art form. We determined to know the perimeters of each prison with considerable more detail than the enemy knew them. Every POW's trip to an interrogation room became a mission to sight, memorize, and report back on specific areas of the prison. We knew every rusty nail that might support a rope or wire. We knew which windows were barred and which were large enough for a man to crawl through. We knew the location of every cell, cell block, guard post, administration building, even the immediate area outside the walls.

Although escape was always in the back of our minds, it wasn't the primary goal of disciplined surveillance. Knowing the intricate details of the prisons had practical day-by-day importance for survival. For example, in July of '66 a new guy, Lt. Commander Cole Black, a neighbor of mine in San Diego, was spotted through a crack in the door in a cell in the Zoo. No one knew that he was down, yet somehow the enemy had him. He wasn't "on the line," didn't know the code. We had to get it to him.

On an earlier surveillance trip, a fellow prisoner had noticed that a clothesline was attached to one end of the new man's cell. Prisoners hanging clothes could whisper the code to Commander Black in segments until he knew it all. From that moment a lot of prisoners used filthy water to wash clothes that would have been better off dirty so that piece by piece the new guy could learn the code and get "on the line." The effort required elaborate preparation and coordination by three different cells, but once again surveillance paid off.

By the time we left that vile prison complex, I could sit down and draw an intricate, detailed description of the entire prison, many sections of which I had never even seen. Surveillance and covert communication helped defeat the

74

enemy's painstaking effort to keep us isolated, confined, and hidden. Isolation is a terrible weapon. Strong men have been destroyed by it. I was constantly amazed at how the loneliness could break my own willingness to resist. Physical torture may have ended, but there is still no torture worse than years of solitary confinement. Our successful struggle to communicate with each other turned a group of prisoners, isolated by cement and steel walls, into a community, and through that community we survived.

Harry Jenkins and I were separated four months later. I spent the last six months of 1970 living alone again. The days after one loses a friend are the hardest days to bear. Immediately I had to develop all kinds of new mental projects to fill those lonely hours. I worked for months trying to recall the names and faces of every member of my high-school graduating class. While trying to remember faces forgotten twenty-four years, I was reminded again how generous God has been in giving man wonderful and mysterious powers.

At night, exhausted from my mental search for high-school friends and asleep at last, I would suddenly awaken with a new name or face recalled. While my body slept, my brain worked on. This computerlike miracle between our ears seems so strong a proof of a loving Father behind creation. In spite of my problems in prison, it became easier to thank God for His gifts. It almost seemed that the less possessions I had, the more significant His really worthwhile gifts became to me.

We didn't have much in the way of possessions during those first five years in prison—a blanket, a pajamalike prison suit, a drinking cup, no Bible (every New Year's Eve for seven years, I repeated my resolution that after my release I would never be without a Bible again), no newspapers. (In fact, I didn't learn that Neil Armstrong had walked on the moon until three years after his return!) We missed pencils and notebooks, and radios and soft pillows, but most of all, I think, we missed decent food—let alone home cooking. Our food was basically the same those first five years. We ate two meals a day. It was either rice or hard French bread with a liter of boiled water. Also, we had a bowl of soup, the rotten cabbage or seaweed varieties, and in the summer sewer greens, little green shoots that grew around sewers. These were thrown on top of the soup, with a piece or two of sowbelly—all fat—plus skin and hair. We didn't eat very high off the hog; you can believe that! Now and then we would get a fish head or tail, all scrap, maybe a hamster, and, if lucky, dog meat or fragged duck. (The men called it "fragged duck" because the duck had been cleavered—bones and all—into tiny fragments.)

Most of what we ate I considered inedible before prison, but meat—even dog meat—is the prime source of protein, and to survive we ate it, hair and all. On special days the enemy might prepare a very edible meal. Usually photographers would be on hand to use our enjoyment of the meal as propaganda, but we all gave in and ate gratefully. On rare occasions a package from home would get through. Everyone would share this unexpected bonanza. If a man got a bottle of vitamins, everyone in camp would get a vitamin that day until the bottle was empty. Our motto was UNITY BEFORE SELF. We shared and in the sharing kept each other alive.

It's important to remember that the North Vietnamese are terribly poor people. Our bombing and blockades had cut down all supplies, including foodstuff; and though we suffered extraordinarily, we weren't the only ones who went to bed hungry in that land.

I lost more than forty pounds in captivity, and I was skinny when captured. The last two years the food increased

New Hope

in quality and quantity. I gained back twenty pounds primarily because the enemy initiated a third meal—the Vietnamese version of breakfast—a cup of hot powdered milk or sugar and a piece of bread. If the war had ended three years earlier, you would have seen a different crew of survivors—skinnier, leaner, and meaner perhaps. That added breakfast those last few years did a lot to mellow us and to fatten us for release.

Perhaps the greatest boost to our morale came during the last few weeks in Stardust. November 21, 1970, the prison and its immediate environs exploded into activity—trucks, troops, and tanks moving in all directions. We saw lights in the night and new construction in the prison. By the evening of November 24, more than two hundred downed American air crews had moved into the western section of the Hanoi Hilton, trucked there blindfolded from camps all around Hanoi.

Finally, we learned what happened that historic night, November 21, 1970. Colonel Bull Simons and his group of seventy had invaded North Vietnam in jet-powered helicopters to search out and rescue prisoners. They landed in the area of Son Tay, about fifteen miles west of Hanoi, and besieged a POW camp there. Unfortunately, at that time there were no Americans being held in that area; but when the word got out that such a mission had taken place, we had concrete evidence that we were not forgotten—that our nation was really trying to bring us home. After that invasion things were never the same at the Hanoi Hilton.

12

Word After Five Years

Phyllis Rutledge
San Diego, California
Thanksgiving, 1970

After John's accident, I went overboard trying to help him. He lay helplessly on his bed, needing total care day and night. I worked around the clock to make him feel comfortable and entertained. If he called, I was there. After all, he was only fifteen years old and needed all the attention I could give him. Besides, I was feeling more and more responsible for the accident. Often, while feeding or bathing my son, I asked myself hard and useless questions. Could the accident have been avoided? If I had been more careful, would John be well today? Will his father think I failed him, that his son is crippled because of my neglect?

The guilty feelings multiplied as I grew tense and overworked. Peggy and Barbara needed more of my time. Sondra was going steady and also needed attention. I was working day and night and gradually falling apart. I knew something had to change as my own frustration mounted to a dangerous level.

All during this time, Pastor Foley and the people of Clairemont First Southern Baptist Church were praying. During the seven years of imprisonment, our family was mentioned in public prayer every Sunday morning faithfully. There were cards and calls of encouragement, cookies and candy for John. I wasn't attending church, but Pastor Foley and his wife still visited often. They didn't berate or badger me. On every visit they would chat a while, share words of encouragement, and say a brief prayer. Then, usually on the way to the door, Brother Foley would invite us to church on Sunday. I never felt pressured. Somehow I knew he understood. Even if we didn't attend, the people at First Church never gave up on us. They were faithful when I wasn't, just as God is faithful when we aren't.

It was my two young ones, Peggy and Barbara, who got me going back to church. They became very active in the youth group and loved singing in the choir. Their enthusiasm was contagious. I went to church when I could be sure John was well taken care of, and the house cleaned, the dishes done, the bills paid, the records kept, the girls ready, and myself presentable. I was trying to do everything and ended up getting more and more irritable with John, impatient with the girls, and angry at myself.

I still didn't know if Howard were alive or dead, and the tension of not hearing anything about my husband for five long years was getting to me. I was trying to be both mom and dad to my growing brood; eventually, I realized that unless something happened I couldn't keep it all together. For a while we had an attendant for John. When he left and my health failed, I had to put John in a nursing home where he could get professional care.

I have to admit that I wasn't aware that God was working in my life during those five years of waiting. But as I look back, it is plain to see that God was working, even then. He was working through people who cared enough to reach out and lift us up. Howard's mother was really used by God to help us survive. She visited us from Tulsa and helped clean up the house, fixed roasts and stews and chocolate pies. She would talk with John and play with the girls. At night, when we couldn't sleep, she would pray and quote promises of hope from the Bible. Before John's accident, she had been the one who noticed him crying during an invitation at church and together they went forward to pray and commit John's life to Christ. He was only eleven, but he and his grandma did important spiritual business that day. No one makes mother-in-law jokes around me anymore. I've seen what a godsend a mother-in-law can be.

LaVerne Barger, one of my Sunday-school teachers at First Church, was another important friend God used. She always seemed to know when I needed her. Invariably she would appear at our door with food or flowers or books just when I was getting low. She and the pastor often visited John and talked with him about the Bible and baseball. Brother Foley once told me that John could ask deeper questions about the Bible than any boy his age. It was good to see my son take an interest in God's Word.

Ken Masat, Howard's wingman who saw his chute that day, also visited John and talked enthusiastically about airplanes and flying. Ken is a Catholic, and I was pleased to learn from him that his church, too, was praying for us.

Other people helped. The city of Bellflower, California, adopted Howard as their prisoner of war and sent the family gifts and gave John a thousand-dollar scholarship.

God was using all kinds of people to help fill the emptiness in our lives, but nothing could really satisfy until we heard from Howard.

Finally, the long, anxiety-ridden silence was broken. About Thanksgiving 1970 I went to my mailbox and pulled out a handfull of bills and fourth-class ads. There was a POW folder and like all the other folders I had gotten I supposed

TRẠI GIAM PHI CÔNG MỸ BỊ BẮT TẠI
NƯỚC VIỆT-NAM DÂN CHỦ CỘNG HÒA
*(Camp of detention for U.S. pilots captured
in the DEMOCRATIC REPUBLIC of VIETNAM)*

NGÀY VIẾT (Dated) 12 October 1970

Dear Phyllis, I had only very minor injury and am today in fair health. I am, therefor, living testimony to the power of your prayers, your love, and faith. I know, in my heart, that you and ours are equally well, and for the same reasons. Keep faith, for we will have our reunion, whether in this world or the next. If you write use this form. Send pictures, gifts. Love all,

CHI CHÚ (N.B.):

1. Phải viết rõ và chỉ được viết trên những dòng kẻ sẵn (*Write legibly and only on the lines*).

2. Gia đình gửi đến cung phải theo dung mau, khuon khó va quy định này (*Notes from families should also conform to this proforma*)

A reproduction of the first letter Phyllis Rutledge received from her husband—five years after he was captured.

it contained news reprints and important speeches about the prisoners or the war. Usually I just opened these folders, skimmed their contents, and tossed them in the trash. This time a strange-looking letter fell out. There were Vietnamese words printed on the cover and inside in a square there were seven beautiful handwritten lines from Howard.

I screamed with delight and ran into the house yelling at the top of my voice, "He's alive. Your daddy is alive." Of course, our joy was tempered slightly by his words "very minor injury." Was he just hiding the truth from us, or was he really well? But the handwriting was obviously his. He was alive for sure. After five years of being suspended between hope and despair, hope tipped the scales.

That Thanksgiving Sunday my family and I took the letter to church and Pastor Foley read it from the pulpit. When he finished reading those seven short lines, he bowed his head and said a prayer of thanks. I will always remember that Thanksgiving and the gratitude I felt to God and to this pastor and friends for the love they had shown to me and my family.

13

Camp Unity

Howard Rutledge
Hanoi Hilton
1971-1972

Pacing my 4 x 8 foot cell in Cell Block Stardust at the Hanoi Hilton, my mind busy recalling a verse of some forgotten hymn, I suddenly remembered this was Christmas Day. My memory flashed to our home in San Diego at Christmas. It had been six years since our family had gathered together around a tree loaded with gifts for a day of food and fun. I pictured Phyllis carrying the Christmas turkey to our table and ten-year-old John jumping up and down, begging to carve it. My daughters Sondra, Peggy, and Barbara, looking beautiful and proud, had set the table in our Christmas finest. How we had enjoyed those feasts together! Earlier that day the children had torn into our endless pile of presents, heaping the torn wrappings into a growing pile, squealing with feigned surprise over gifts they had spied out earlier, hidden in closets and underneath their parents' bed.

Six years had passed since our family had been together around the Christmas tree, and my eyes filled with tears prompted by those happy memories; but in my cell that day, I was astounded to realize how unware I had been of the real meaning of Christmas on those days so long ago. Oh, I knew it was Christ's birthday and I knew He was God's Son—Someone very special. That was nice, but it took prison to help me to see what Christmas really meant. All the world was a prison, and every man a prisoner until He came. On that night two thousand years ago, God had invaded my world. Like Colonel Bull Simons and his brave group of seventy, God came down to search out and rescue prisoners. Baby Jesus, lying in a filthy manger, surrounded by the smells and sounds of the barnyard, was more than a cute, cuddly kid, as Christmas cards portray Him. He was God Himself come down. He would grow to manhood. He would risk His life to break open prison doors. He would die to set men free. Christmas Day would be the beginning of freedom for men who would believe. I spent that day thinking of the freedom I felt in Christ and wishing to be free to celebrate His birth again with my family.

That Christmas night my devotional reveries were disturbed by the sounds of guards entering Las Vegas, throwing open cell-block doors. Without warning all of us in Las Vegas were herded one-by-one out of that stinking place and into one large area we promptly dubbed Camp Unity. Talk about a celebration! We laughed and hugged and chatted excitedly. We had no idea why we were together or what it meant— but we were together. And if it were only for a night, we would enjoy it.

Up to that point I had spent fifty-eight months in solitary confinement with only a few short breaks; that is 1,740 days alone. Other men had spent over four years in solitary, too; and here we were, milling about in a big room, shaking hands with men we had known and loved for years—men we knew intimately, yet had never seen. For years it had taken as much as twenty-four hours to get a message around that crowd and twenty-four hours to get the answer back. Men had risked and suffered much to communicate a sentence in a day. Now,

84

Here we were milling about in a big room, shaking hands with men we had known and loved for years.

suddenly, we were face-to-face. Everybody wanted to talk to everybody else simultaneously. It was a wild and happy Christmas night.

The enemy had gathered all the downed American air-crews into this one prison. There were nine cell blocks around Camp Unity. Each of them had about forty men. One of the first things we did in Camp Unity was to begin regular church services in every cell block. In the past five years we had sent covert devotional messages from cell to cell, but now we would sit down and worship together in groups. We sang a hymn, someone quoted Scripture, another prayed, a third man shared a meditation. Everything was from memory. There were no hymnbooks, no Bibles, no pews. The service was imperfect but beautiful and very important to our morale. Almost every prisoner entered into worship whole-heartedly.

The enemy immediately decided that church services would be interrupted and the worshippers disbanded. To the North Vietnamese, most of whom didn't speak our language, this was a political meeting. Asians, friends and foes alike, use singing and speeches in group gatherings like our church services for political purposes. Our service was immediately suspected of being a dangerous rallying point. Of course, we tried to explain that we had assembled simply to worship God. We even invited the English-speaking enemy officers to join us in our service so that they would convince our guards that this was church and nothing else. They refused.

The pressure to discontinue worship mounted. Though the torture had ended, threats were made. Reprisals were prom-ised. The guards would heckle us, trying to drown out the words of those who led—but we refused to give up our right to worship God. It seemed the most natural and proper issue on which to take our stand. We enjoyed this new taste of communal life, but we would risk the privilege to keep our

86

right to worship together. A slowdown was inevitable.

The cell blocks in Camp Unity were divided more or less by seniority. I was in the senior cell block during that first wonderful month of communal living. We knew that if the enemy had to be confronted with our right to hold church services on Sunday morning, that confrontation would be our task. So, for two weeks we invited the Vietnamese (those who spoke English and their officers) to join us in church to see what we were doing and to prove we were doing nothing to endanger the internal security of their prison. They continued to refuse, and by the third Sunday the confrontation was imminent.

February 7, 1971, all the guards in camp hung around the senior cell block. This was it. George Coker, the young navy lieutenant from Alcatraz, was acting as the chaplain in our cell block that Sunday. He was the junior officer in the building, yet it was his morning to conduct the service and address the group. We had a small choir to sing a familiar hymn. I was going to recite the 101st Psalm, and Lt. Colonel Risner was going to lead the benediction.

As we began the morning's hymn, the doors opened, and the guards poured in. We had already decided to continue the worship at any cost, and we all looked straight at Lieutenant Coker as he spoke. The guards tried to keep him quiet. They argued and cursed; Lieutenant Coker just kept talking.

Then it was my turn. The guards tried to interfere in every way they could short of physical abuse. I continued quoting Psalm 101; they kept yelling for me to stop. The choir sang and Lt. Colonel Risner gave the benediction prayer. By now the guards were embarrassed and angry and determined to have revenge.

The service ended, but no one moved except the guards who stalked out angrily. The "church riot" had been heard by everyone, and we all awaited for the ax to fall. Fifteen minutes passed before the guards returned. Then they re-entered Cell Block 7 and called out Lieutenant Coker, Lt. Colonel Risner, and myself; the three of us were herded into the courtyard just outside the cell-block gate.

Everyone watched as we nervously awaited our fate. I must confess the memories of past torture and abuse were still vivid in my mind. What did the enemy have planned? What would that short service cost us?

As we stood, each alone with his own questions, each handling his own anxieties, a fantastic thing happened. Somewhere in Cell Block 7 someone began to sing the first verse of "The Star-Spangled Banner." It had not been sung (on penalty of severe punishment) for five long years, but somewhere, someone was singing it. Others joined in. Before one line had passed, all of Cell Block 7 was alive with that song; and by the time the officer returned to march us away, it seemed that every cell block in Camp Unity was singing.

O say, can you see, by the dawn's early light,
What so proudly we hailed at the twilight's last gleaming,
Whose broad stripes and bright stars, through the perilous
    fight,
O'er the ramparts we watched were so gallantly streaming?
And the rockets' red glare, the bombs bursting in air,
Gave proof through the night that our flag was still there;
O say, does that Star-Spangled Banner yet wave
O'er the land of the free and the home of the brave?

There was a lump in my throat as we were marched away from our friends, the sounds of the national anthem ringing through that old French prison in Hanoi. Of course, we had no idea where we were going or what we would find when we got there. So that march and the months that followed were torturous. Alone again after a taste of communal living, locked in Heartbreak-sized small cells, forced to communicate covertly again was torture, indeed. But we had conquered! From that Sunday until the prisoners were released, church services were held throughout the prison with little, if any, interference from the enemy.

Junior officers remained in communal-living status for the rest of their imprisonment, but the senior officers were eventually locked into what we called Building Zero. When Lt. Colonel Risner and I arrived in Zero, we found small cells, appalling filth, and extreme heat. At least ten men were in irons; sometimes two on a bunk. They weren't permitted out and had to perform all their bodily functions with their legs shackled to the slab. Lt. Colonel Risner and I were not in irons, so we set about to clear the guards, begin communications, and raise the spirits of the men who suffered there.

Here in Building Zero—code name Rawhide—I talked for the first time through closed doors to Col. John Flynn, the senior prisoner in North Vietnam. John is an extremely strong yet sensitive man and proved an outstanding leader. He had been informed of the church riot in Cell Block 7 and had decided for us to have church in Building Zero. Remember, Rawhide imprisoned men in cells, isolated from each other, shackled in solitary or small groups; but Colonel Flynn knew how much even a brief time of prayer and worship would mean.

We plotted carefully to clear the area and conduct the service. Robby Risner prayed a magnificent prayer, and I quoted imperfectly but with enthusiasm, the 101st Psalm; Jack Finley, an air force lieutenant colonel, whistled "Ave Maria." I don't remember hearing anything so beautiful in my life as Jack's version of that great old Catholic song. We worshipped regularly in Rawhide in spite of barriers of brick and cement; in fact, we even formed a choir with individual members separated by their cells. Those men could really

sing. We were all denominations. All the things that could
have divided us didn't matter in Building Zero. We were
united in our faith in God and in each other. Nothing else
mattered.

March 19, 1971, I moved into a 6 x 7 foot cell with my old
and great friends Harry Jenkins, Jim Stockdale, and Jerry
Denton. There were only two concrete bunks, no ventilation,
no windows; we were four men locked together in a room
with little or no space to walk; it was hot and filthy and
crowded. Each of us carefully organized his daily schedule,
trying to be sensitive to each other without giving up the
discipline, physical and mental, long established. It was easy
to be irritable. None of us had any saintly inclinations. There
were harsh words and embarrassing silences, but we were
united against a common enemy. The enemy was more than
ignorant and abusive guards. The enemy was loneliness and
fear and death. We would survive, and we would survive
with honor. Any anger or impatience between us quickly dis-
solved in our common task—to survive—and in our love for
one another.

I never stopped doing my daily routines. Some part of
each day was filled with Scripture recall. We worked together
to find more. Every man found some floating in his memory
and contributed to the pile. Daily I would pray for my
family, and renew my resolve to make my commitment to
Christ, and join my family's church upon return to freedom.
In prison I firmly believed that there was a God who loved
me and was working in my life. I cannot explain with reason
or proof why my faith was central to my survival. But it was.
Other men went in unbelieving and came out the same. I
didn't, and for me my faith in Christ made all the difference.

Somehow we all survived that long hot summer '71, and
in September, nine of us were moved into Cell Block 8. These
were the nine senior officers under Colonel Flynn. We had

already organized the cell blocks into a complete, sophisticated command structure much like an air force wing command, with Colonel Flynn as the wing commander. Every building in our covert communications system was given a code name. If the enemy intercepted our traffic, he had no idea what it meant, who originated it, or who was to receive the message. Cell Block 8 became our headquarters. We gave it code name BLUE. The wing commander's code was SKY. So any men who received a message from SKY BLUE knew that Wing Commander Flynn was sending it from headquarters.

My responsibility as wing communications officer was to keep communications open, to keep every man "on the line." If we could keep every man alert and informed, he would not fall to angry interrogators pushing for propaganda statements or military information. When one man went to interrogation, we all knew immediately and sent waves of support in his direction. We were working at maximal resistance and had one united goal: RELEASE WITH HONOR. We wanted to leave that place as men, standing tall and proud, not broken and bent. Our goal was to produce men who had more than survived—men who had conquered.

Besides promoting mental activity, the wing worked to get us back in good physical health. Every man ate everything he could. Exercise programs were part of the wing's organization, and even those men with broken bones worked hard to get and keep their bodies in shape. Cellmates would walk their rooms for miles a day in line, do push-ups, sit-ups, and run in place. The organization worked to get us ready for that day we hoped lay ahead—*Freedom!*

Remember, all our communications were still covert. It took time and effort. The enemy knew of this underground wing organization and did everything short of physical torture to chop communications and kill our system. But the enemy could not stop us. It was a great and exciting effort on the part of many men that kept our wing command strong and effective during those last long months of imprisonment.

Moving then, in September of '71, was a big move up for all of us. It was the first time in six years that I had been in a cell with an open window—there were bars, but it was a window. It wasn't dark in that cell, and now and then breezes made breathing bearable. In fact, often in the daytime we were allowed into a small 12 x 12 foot courtyard area for two or three hours a day; for the first time in 75 months I felt the sunshine on my face. The walls around me were 15 feet high and broken glass was imbedded in their surface, but I could look up past those walls and see the sun. It was a glorous sight.

We even had a kind of Vietnamese toilet. It was only a hole with a squatting place, but it was a luxury. I still dreamed of beautiful white toilet seats, white pillow cases, a soft bed with clean sheets, and chocolate-covered peanuts! We weren't home yet, and the conditions, though improved, were still frightful by any standards. There were still the mosquitoes, the insects, the lice, the parasites that lived on and in our bodies, and the rats that surprised us by nibbling on our toes at night.

As I was stretched out on my hardwood bed in Cell Block 8 one night, I was awakened by the feeling that something was gnawing on the end of my thumb. It was a rat the size of a small opossum; and when I yelled, I scared him as much as he had scared me. Unfortunately, we were both trapped in my mosquito net. We rolled together biting and bashing, but with the help of my cellmates, I finally did him in. Those experiences look funny to me now. They didn't then!

My friends in prison had all been Americans until Cell Block 8. There I met three outstanding men from Thailand

and one South Vietnamese pilot, allies shot down, captured, and imprisoned like ourselves. The South Vietnamese could speak English, French, Spanish and Thai. He was a brilliant young man, an able friend and conspirator against the enemy. The Thais were industrious and friendly, but they couldn't speak English, so at first we couldn't communicate. I must confess at first we were suspicious of them because we didn't know who or what they were. As trustees who worked around the compound, they had access to all our secrets. We watched and waited and wondered if they were friends or foes. Then one day the South Vietnamese pilot spoke out.

"Commander, do you trust me?" he asked through the wall that separated us.

I didn't hestitate. "Of course, I trust you. We are allies. You were shot down fighting with us. Why shouldn't I trust you?"

He paused and then continued. "If you trust me," he said, "know this; the three Thais are true and loyal friends. You must trust them too."

That ended the matter, and immediately we set about teaching the Thais English and the code. They learned them both, and we were constantly amazed and grateful for their skills and friendship. We always ended our communications in code throughout the wing sending R.W.H.S.W.D.G.B.U!, which translates: RELEASE WITH HONOR. STICK WITH DICK. GOD BLESS YOU!

The Thais were Buddhists, and I was surprised to get a message one day that ended with the part of that sign-off that they could not really understand: GOD BLESS YOU! On Christmas and Easter I had spent time tapping out the meaning of these holidays. Perhaps they had understood.

We worked hard those last months of 1972, contacting new people, maintaining our organization, and operating covertly inside of the Hoa Lo prison complex. People may wonder why we didn't attempt to escape. Unfortunately, they believe that prison life is like the world of "Hogan's Heroes," that slapstick television series featuring imaginary American prisoners in World War II.

There had been at least two attempts by Americans to escape from North Vietnamese prisons. George McKnight and Lieutenant Coker earned their way to Alcatraz through their escape from Dirty Bird, October 1, 1967. Ed Atterberry and John Dramesi escaped from the Zoo, May 10, 1969, but were recaptured shortly and brought back to that prison in the same truck. There they shook hands, wished each other luck and were parted. No one has ever seen Ed Atterberry again.

There were heavy reprisals for escape attempts; and though we thought about it, diagrammed the area, and made various plans in '71 and '72, our plans were never tried. We were locked in cells, inside of cell blocks, inside of a series of jagged glass and hot-wire walls, in a massive prison with inner and outer walls, with twenty-four-hour guard surveillance, in the heart of the capital city. Even if a prisoner survived an escape he would have no friends and no place to hide in downtown Hanoi. So, until 1973 we waited for the miracle of freedom to happen from the outside. One day we would be taken through the gates of the Hanoi Hilton to freedom or to death. Until that day we had to pray and work and wait.

14

Help For John

Phyllis Rutledge
San Diego, California,
1971-1972

The letter from Howard around Thanksgiving, 1970, had assured me he was alive physically. Subsequent mail told me he was alive again spiritually. I thanked God for His wonderful double blessing.

In the next two years, there were only a dozen or so other letters from Howard, but it was easy to read between the lines. My husband's Christian life was growing. He had shown almost no spiritual leadership in our home in the past twenty years, but it sounded as if something had happened to him to change all that. It got me thinking about my own spiritual growth. I began to read the Bible. I read books on prayer, and I began to pray again. The family went to church regularly and found our real friends were there. People like Virginia Smith and Yvonne Boling were quick to help out in a crisis and never expected to be thanked for their thoughtfulness. I don't know what I would have done without the people at First Church.

I was pretty well on top of things except for John. He was really losing ground in the nursing home. Surrounded by old people who were dying, constantly aware of the sadness and despair around him, John's morale was sinking fast. One afternoon I walked out of the nursing home knowing that if I didn't get him out of there soon, we would lose our son. I was afraid he might get on drugs or even try suicide. He had every reason to be depressed. But I had no idea where to take him.

The next morning I decided something must be done. In Sunday-school class one of my friends had told of a recent experience when she and her family "let Jesus take them out to dinner." It may sound farfetched, but they got into their car and asked God to lead them to a restaurant. They drove through the streets of La Jolla, turning down one street and up another. Then they felt it was time to stop. There was a restaurant nearby that they had never tried. So they went in, had a wonderful evening, a delicious meal, paid the bill, and thanked God for His guidance.

So I thought to myself, "What can I lose?" If God cares about dinner, surely He cares about my son's suffering! I'll try trusting God to lead me to a place that can help John. So I got up, got dressed, climbed into the car, and prayed for guidance. There was a new rehabilitation center nearby and it seemed natural to start there. So, I drove towards Clairemont Mesa Boulevard and Sharps Hospital. I got out of the car, walked into the brand-new reception area, and to my surprise found John's doctor in the corridor as if waiting for me. I don't know about your experience trying to catch a doctor in, but this was something new for me.

I walked up to Dr. A. J. Russell and said, "I have to talk with you."

Surprised, he answered, "Fine, !" We sat down on a bench, and I told him my fears about John's living in that place, surrounded by death and the dying, growing more and more depressed.

He answered with concern. "I've just been talking with

some old med-school friends of mine who are starting an experimental rehabilitation center for young people in Tempe, Arizona. I'll call them about John, and we'll see what they can do." I mumbled words of thanks and made a hasty retreat from the hospital.

I don't pretend my faith was strong. I didn't even know for sure he would call me back. But he did, and not long after, John was flown to Tempe, Arizona, and the Good Samaritan Rehabilitation Center. It was a miracle, and it came just in time. And though he is still paralyzed, today he is studying at University of California at Berkeley.

Thanks to God and all the people who cared, we were making headway. I even got the checkbook balanced now and then. But the big question remained. When would the war end so that Howard could come home?

POW AND MIA wives around the country were beginning to feel that it might never end. We organized our small informal groups into a national organization and worked to keep the prisoners' plight before the public. It's easy to forget a man when he has been in prison seven years. We could not let the public forget.

The National League of Families of POW and MIA in Southeast Asia worked hard writing congressmen, the military, and the press. Other groups sold bracelets with the prisoner's name, rank, and date of capture to raise money to help our cause and, again, to keep our men remembered. Thousands of people wore those bracelets. Hundreds of them wrote me that they were praying for Howard and for his safe return.

As the talks in Paris continued and Dr. Kissinger dashed around the world, we held our breath and prayed for our president. He was only human and had a superhuman task to perform. Like all of us, he would make mistakes, but he tried, as we were trying, to get our men home again.

One Christmas would come and go, and we would say, "Next Christmas they'll be home." Then another twelve months would slowly pass with no real hope in sight. I tried to be casual about the whole thing, but my excitement mounted as the talks in Paris and the secret visits to Peking, Moscow, and Hanoi were made known. Then, unbelievably, the peace was signed! Howard would soon be home!

15

Going Home

Howard Rutledge
Gia Lam Airport, Hanoi
February 11, 1973

On January 31, 1973, it seemed our prayers for freedom had been answered. Still living in Cell Block 8, we had learned of the agreement signed in Paris three days before. As an important part of that agreement, the United States had demanded that the North Vietnamese deliver into prisoner hands a copy of the protocol describing our release. When we heard the news, Colonel Flynn asked the nine of us to stop our work so that we could thank God for His mercy. We had hoped and prayed for so long; now freedom was in sight. We didn't say much. I suppose we didn't have to. A look of relief and joy was on everybody's face. I am sure the good Lord could look into our hearts and see the gratitude that was there as we prayed.

I had never prayed much after dropping out of church twenty years before—never with Phyllis. But in prison many of my most important memories are associated with prayer. There were dramatic prayers like the one Colonel Risner prayed, with the enemy cursing and yelling at him during the church riot of '71. There were prayers of great sadness like those prayers we prayed for our comrade dying and alone in Alcatraz. There were even funny prayers. One example I recall occurred in Cell Block 7. We were digging a hole between two cell blocks to help us communicate by voice between them; unfortunately the hole had to be dug with the diggers lying in the latrine. The smell was terrible. One day at grace John Dramesi prayed, "God, help them get that hole dug through the latrine before it's my turn to dig again." Talking to God became a natural process, like eating and breathing.

There were eloquent prayers by men like Commander Chuck Gillespie or Col. Norman Gaddis or Col. Dave Winn who were strong Christians and who had obviously developed seasoned prayer lives, but praying was a new experience for me. I'm still not very good at it. Words don't come easy when I pray. But even we amateurs discovered in prison the incredibly powerful force prayer can be in our lives. I learned I could talk to God anyplace, dangling from a parachute or shackled in a cesspool. I learned He could hear me whether in worship with a crowd of men or alone in solitary confinement. I learned He understood even if I fumbled for the words, spoke with rotten grammer, or asked Him to do crazy, unreasonable things.

There was a time when I might have thought that men who prayed a lot were milquetoasts or sissy types. Now I know differently. There were times I thought prayer was a silly ritual we did from guilt or pressure, an act of piety we performed in church, or family worship that really didn't have much meaning. Now I know the truth. Prayer really works! I still don't pray aloud very well. But I have tested prayer and found God hears and answers. So when Colonel Flynn, the senior officer in Vietnam, asked us to stop and pray, it seemed the right and natural thing to do.

February 6, 1973, we were moved together into a large room in Cell Block 6. It was there I met for the first time since our capture Denny Moore, a man from my old Squadron, who had been shot down exactly one month before I was. I thought he was dead until I learned he was being held in a cell block next to mine. To walk up to Denny and say, "Hello! Glad you are alive," to shake hands again with old friends separated for years by iron and cement was a real thrill.

We enjoyed a lot of things about Cell Block 6. I played my first volleyball game in seven years in prison; I spent wonderful hours in long conversations with old and new friends, and we had great spiritual experiences there. We gathered for worship. Howie Dunn, a marine lieutenant colonel, led a five- or six-man choir that was terrific (by now choirs were common to all the cell blocks, and on an average Sunday one could hear hymns of praise echoing through that entire prison complex).

Norm McDaniels, a very profound and sincere, black air force officer, led the worship and preached the morning meditation. He had been in a cell block where a Bible had been available for a short time, and he quoted a psalm. Then he spoke to each of us. We knew this might be our last service in prison. His subject was right on target. Being a pilot himself, he knew that none of us had ever gone into combat thinking we would be shot down, captured and imprisoned, certainly not for seven long years. Now that release was in sight, he knew we all were asking, "Why me?" He listed the reasons many of us had already been thinking. "Am I here because I have committed some ugly sin and God is punishing me for it?" Am I here as a test of faith, a trial by fire?" "Or is it all a mistake? I accidentally got in the way of enemy fire and now God's helping me make the best of it." Each of us had to come to terms with these questions.

As I looked into my own life, I thought, "Yes, I was a sinner," and, "Yes, this has been a test of my faith," and, "Yes,

God has really helped to bring something to me from those long prison years." After all, I was shot down, a church dropout, disinterested in Christian truth. I would return to freedom aware of God and anxious to stay "on the line" with Him.

Earlier in the service we had sung the Doxology.

> Praise God from whom all blessings flow;
> Praise Him, all creatures here below;
> Praise Him above, ye heavenly host;
> Praise Father, Son, and Holy Ghost.

Norm McDaniels ended his closing prayer; the choir sang the benediction hymn:

> Hear our prayer, O Lord,
> Hear our prayer, O Lord,
> Incline Thine ear to us,
> And grant us Thy peace.

Sunday, February 11, 1973, was the end of the two-week period outlined in the protocol we had received. We arose that morning wondering if this might be the day. That afternoon the North Vietnamese chopped up eight turkeys and fed them to the 200 airmen in that prison. Having turkey was not common to everyday life. Our excitement mounted.

At sunset the guards entered our cell blocks and took us, six or seven at a time, to Heartbreak. There was a moment of fear as the first group entered that ugly place filled with so many terrible memories, but quickly our spirits soared as we were issued new clothing for release. There were 115 of us chosen for this first increment, and now we had our clothing ready and our release bags packed. Sitting around that night, unable to sleep, we felt the next day to be almost anticlimactic by that time.

We were going to leave as we had come—*with. dignity*. We would go home with honor! The torture had ended; we had kept the faith. Finally, the sun rose above Hanoi. No gong was needed to get that crew of excited airmen up and dressed for this occasion. We were going home!

By 8 A.M. we were lined up outside our cells. A guard checked off our names, and we walked out of the gates of the Hanoi Hilton. There were six buses waiting. We watched and waited as the men on stretchers were loaded and driven away towards Gia Lam Airport. Then the rest of us, less ill, wounds almost healed, climbed on board with heads high. It was the first time in seven years that I had sat in a vehicle without my hands in rear cuffs and my eyes blindfolded. I watched the prison through my window as we pulled away. It had been a kind of tomb for seven years, and now I felt resurrected from the dead, driving away to life again.

Hanoi was in ruins. It is a poverty-stricken place—hard to describe. Long years of war had taken an effective toll. The city was a mess, but the streets were alive with people. Apparently the news of our release had been broadcast over Radio Hanoi. The people lined the streets, stopped their work, and watched as we drove by. There were many friendly gestures and happy waves. Everyone was smiling, obviously aware of our great joy. We didn't smile back.

When we arrived at the airport, we didn't feel particularly joyful. There were no airplanes. The airport was bombed and gutted. On one of the few buildings that remained, a Red Cross flag was flying—the first we had seen in seven years. We unloaded the buses. Our guards told us that there would be a delay as both sides hammered out the final details of the turnover.

We stood around nervously. At first there were feeble attempts at joking about our predicament. Then we lapsed into silence. About noon the Vietnamese brought us something to drink and some stale sandwiches. We ate them, hoping this was our last meal in Vietnam. No one wanted any trouble. There was too much to lose. We wanted the release to go smoothly. Others were still in prison and our actions could affect their release.

We could see the international control teams scurrying around. There was nothing to do but wait. Suddenly the guards loaded us back on the buses and we drove towards loading ramps on the runway. A cheer went up as the first C-141 transport broke through the overcast and landed. By now each of us calculated in his mind how many men per plane we would pull. It was obvious that I would be on the second C-141. It had not appeared, and as the first plane was loaded, I just knew there would be no second plane—that I would end up driving back through Hanoi to spend more time in prison.

Then the second C-141 broke through the haze and made its final approach. Suddenly the pilot added power and went back up again. I knew perfectly well this wasn't some new form of torture, but oh, how it hurt to see that plane fly by! We sweated his second approach inch by inch; and when he was finally down, we allowed ourselves a cheer. We knew now that in minutes our nightmare would be over.

The first C-141 taxied out and took off toward Clark Air Force Base in the Philippines. Then it was our turn. An especially hated North Vietnamese officer—nicknamed Slick or Soft Soap Ferry—came to our bus with a binder containing a list of names. He was one of the most dangerous men I had ever seen, known as a consummate liar and an extortioner, guilty of torture and death, and personally responsible for a great deal of our misery. There he was, calling out names. I am sure every man that crossed the line to freedom felt a flash of bitterness as Slick called each name.

We saluted the air force colonel standing there.

Then we were walking towards the ramp. We saluted the air force colonel standing there, and one by one we were escorted to the plane. I shivered when I finally stood inside that beautiful rescue ship. Harry Jenkins and I chose the last seat in the plane and slumped gratefully into its cushions for the long ride home.

16

"Hello, Phyllis?"

Howard Rutledge
Clark Air Force Base,
February 12, 1973

A few hours in an airplane can seem an eternity to a prisoner homeward bound. Fortunately, the first hours were filled with pleasant new sights and sounds on the C-141 that carried us. This was a medic plane, and it was manned inside by a couple of beautiful American flight nurses. We hadn't seen American women for more than seven years. I must confess that all of us, including me, just stared at them with delight as they arranged our pillows and plied us with creature comforts. Their bright smiles and sweet smells after seven years of living in an all-male prison, with the smell of death in the air, were almost too much to bear.

Early in the flight we flew over the attack carrier *Enterprise* on maneuvers in the South China Sea. An old friend, Jack Christianson, was the carrier division commander now just a few thousand feet below. There was a moment of silence as we passed that beautiful ship. There wasn't a man aboard our plane who wouldn't have given his right arm to be down there operating that great carrier. All of us were professionals, and it felt so good to be back in our own world of ships and planes and pilots.

The sleek new C-141 that was carrying us provided another source of inspiration and conversation for a bunch of old flyers who had almost lost touch with their profession —in my case, for the last seven years. In fact, the airplane, the pilot and copilot had all been commissioned after I was shot down. The copilot wasn't even in high school when I was taken captive and here he was the one chosen to fly us home! I felt a bit like Rip Van Winkle waking up in the middle of an unfamiliar world. While I had been locked away in a concrete prison cell, the world had changed. My children had grown up, graduated, married, had children of their own, and I had missed it all. Men had gone to school, won their wings, flown their missions and been given commands while I had paced beneath a prison wall. It wasn't long before the cheering and the celebrating died down, and we were left alone with our memories and our questions.

What would we face at home? Who had died? Who had gone away? Men thought of wives, sweethearts, friends, parents. Many were flying home to face divorce or death in their families. Others would require extensive hospitalization; some needed surgery. There were broken bones to be reset, teeth that needed care. Many needed counseling. We all needed rest. What tragic surprises would greet us? Could we face the coming days? Could we begin again?

What would we face in America? We had heard about the antiwar activities, the demonstrations, and marches. I felt some anger at those who had opposed the war; but I had been fighting to defend their right to oppose it. But how would they feel about me now? Would we be booed in the streets? Would our families be humiliated, our children scorned? We had no idea of what our reception would be.

It was a long flight home, but all too soon it ended. The wheels touched down on the runways of Clark Air Force Base, the Philippines. We had no idea of the reception that

It wasn't long before the cheering and the celebrating died down, and we were left alone with our memories and our questions.

awaited us.

Harry and I hung back as the men deplaned. I was the last one to leave the C-141, and imagine my surprise at our reception. There was a long red carpet, a clear sign of welcome known round the world. At the head of that carpet stood Admiral Noel Gayler, Commander in Chief of the Pacific. If we had had any fears about our reception, they ended in that bus ride to Clark Hospital. The road was lined with children and adults. They carried hand-painted signs: WELCOME HOME! GOD BLESS YOU! YOU HAVE KEPT THE FAITH! It seems like a dream now—the friendly smiles —the children waving, held high on Father's shoulders— women crying—and young people cheering.

We arrived at the hospital at dinnertime and immediately got in line. The men who had arrived on the first flight were standing in hospital pajamas and wearing LIGHT DIET tags pinned to their shirts. They were glumly receiving their bowls of soup, jello and custard when we stepped up to order steaks, and pie, and banana splits. The flawless planning of Operation Homecoming had included special diets for us all. But we had not received our tags, and needless to say, the medical officer saw that all of us could stand the shock of good American cooking, so he tore up the light diet order and we all dug in.

For three days we remained at Clark Air Force Base, and I suspect my total amount of sleep was less than three hours in that entire period. It was time to be debriefed. The names and serial numbers we had memorized were taken down by debriefing officers and compared, one list against the other. If there were men still in prison and not on the lists, our government was determined to find them. They wanted to know everything we knew about how many Americans were still in prison. What was their condition? Who were missing? Who had died?

"Hello, Phyllis?"

At last I was alone in my hospital room, and the operator on my bedside phone informed me that my call to America and my family was ready. I had received only four cards of the hundreds of letters and packages she had mailed. I had waited six years before I received that first seven-line card the enemy finally granted me. Phyllis was on the line seven thousand miles away. What would she say? How would she feel about me?

"Hello, Phyllis?"

That warm voice of the woman I love, with her slight Oklahoma drawl, was full of love and welcome. She tried to put my mind at ease that everyone was well and waiting anxiously for my return. But I could sense she was holding back. Finally, she told me of my son John's accident four years before. He had been swimming with friends near our home in La Jolla and had dived into the ocean and struck his head against a rock hidden just beneath the surface. Phyllis told me quietly, calmly that he had been permanently paralyzed from the neck down but was as smart and witty as ever and couldn't wait to see his dad. Finally, after talking briefly to my daughters and learning some happy news about my grandson, I hung up and tried to sleep.

My mind went back to George Air Force Base, Victorville, California. John was only two years old when we were stationed there. One hot summer afternoon I went with him to an ice-cream truck; we bought a half-dozen frozen popsicles. He ran excitedly in front of me back into the house. We had a powerful air cooler that kicked up quite a suction draft. As Johnny went through the door, the suction slammed it shut on his hand. I dropped those popsicles, yanked open the door, and wrapped his finger, dangling by a thread of skin, in the palm of my hand. Phyllis drove us to the emergency hospital, and the surgeon spent more than an hour sewing Johnny's little finger back on his hand.

I paced the hospital waiting room, reliving that moment, seeing the door slam, hearing his cries of pain. I would gladly have given every finger on both my hands to save my son's precious little finger. When the doctors finally came in, they said we had very little chance that he would use it again. But when a child is two years old, miracles often happen, and the finger grew back. By the time he was ten, Johnny was one great Little Leaguer.

Now he lay paralyzed from the neck down. But for a miracle, John would never move again. That night in Clark I would gladly have taken the next flight back to Hanoi and locked myself in Heartbreak if it would have given Johnny the use of his arms and legs. It was like being locked away again in solitary, powerless to change what desperately needed changing.

God had been so real to me in prison. This time when I prayed, there was no clear answer. I don't understand these things. I don't know why God seems to intervene so plainly in one event and seems so absent in another. But I refuse to let my questions overpower my faith in Him. To not believe there is a God at work in the world is a grim and unacceptable option. I do believe God is working in John's life just as he is working in mine. He has a plan for both of us. Now, John and I would have to find it together.

17

AFTER SEVEN YEARS

Phyllis Rutledge
San Diego, California,
February 12, 1973

On Sunday, January 28, 1973, I learned that Howard would soon be released, I rushed down to the church, told Pastor Foley that this would be our day, and then rushed home to await further news. Again, the church service stopped and the people thanked God together for answer to prayer. Every time the phone rang, I thought I'd faint with excitement. First, it was Howard's mom calling from Tulsa. She had just hung up, disappointed that there had been no more news, when the phone rang again. The navy was calling to officially notify me that Howard was to be included in the first group coming out of Hanoi.

I didn't let myself get too excited. He wasn't free yet. All we had been told was that he would be flown to Clark Air Force Base in the Philippines. We were also told that there would be no press there, but that we would be sent a picture immediately when he arrived.

Two weeks passed. They were the longest weeks of my life. Would Howard be the same? How had prison changed him? Would he be well? How would he react when I told him of John's accident and paralysis? Would he blame me?

Would he approve of the new house I had bought and of the way I had managed the ledger he gave me seven years ago?

Then my phone rang again. An excited neighbor reported the first plane was landing at Clark. The girls ran to the television, and together we watched the first load of men climb down. No Howard. Our phone was ringing off the hook. The people at First Church had been praying seven years, and they really got involved in their praying. Now in homes all over the neighborhood, they were waiting to see the man they had been praying for. We were all going crazy with excitement by the time the second plane landed.

Thirty-nine men got off, one by one they said their words of thanks, saluted the military officers, then walked the long red carpet to freedom. Still no Howard. Then a slender, black-haired man climbed off the plane. The newsman's voice grew silent. Then we heard him say, with a kind of laugh, "Captain Howard Rutledge; he says his name is Howie."

A cheer that God couldn't help but hear went up that day from the Rutledge house and from the houses of the people of First Church. A thousand voices hoarse with hollering, two thousand hands back-slapping, and a thousand people dancing with joy around their living rooms! Howard's home! I'm sure that God knew that those cheers were our way of saying thanks for bringing Howard home.

The cameras were close. We all saw him clearly. He looked thin, but he was walking, head high; and when he saluted Admiral Gayler, we could tell he was all right. He called me three times from the Philippines during the next three days. Each time it was about 3 A.M., I think. He talked very low and very slowly. And the conversations were a bit strained. You know how it is when you've been storing up things to say for years, and then when it's time to say them, you freeze with excitement.

114

When I finally had the courage to tell him about John, he paused for one long moment. Then he spoke. "Phyllis, do you blame yourself for Johnny's accident?" I mumbled something tearfully; then slowly, calmly, as though we were back on that bed the midnight I had seen him last, he said, "Phyllis, I trust you in all things. I know you did your very best. That's all anyone can ask."

I learned a lot about God that day. "I can do all things through Christ which strengtheneth me." (Philippians 4:13).

18

SOME RESOLUTIONS

Howard Rutledge
San Diego, California
February 16, 1973

The next morning a young hospital orderly passed me the third note from one of the nurses saying she would like an interview. Security at Clark was at a maximum. We ex-POWs had determined among ourselves not to speak of prison life or conditions to anyone until all the other men were free. But this note was accompanied by a scribbled sentence from the orderly: YOU'D BETTER SEE HER, SIR. SHE'S VERY PRETTY.

So, curious, I asked the orderly to bring the nurse to the waiting room on my floor. I'll not forget that meeting. The orderly was right. Miss Ronalyn Thompson was very pretty. She also had a gift for me. It was an aluminum bracelet with my name, rank, and the date of my captivity printed on it. I'll never forget what she said when she gave me my bracelet that afternoon.

"Captain Rutledge, for many months I've worn your bracelet, without taking it off night or day. Every day I've prayed for your safe return. Now these prayers are answered. I just wanted to tell you how glad I am you're home again." Then she was gone. Later I learned that millions of

Americans, young and old, from all walks of life, had been wearing ID bracelets like this one to keep the memories of the POW and MIA men clear in the public's mind and to remind them daily to pray for our safe return. I believe those prayers had everything to do with my return and, again, I am grateful.

The last leg of that journey home began February 15 as our giant transport flew towards San Diego and reunion with the ones we loved. There was so much I wanted to tell my family. There was even more I wanted to hear from them. In prison I had plenty of time to decide on the things I wanted to change in my life.

I had gone away a church dropout. I was returning transformed by what I'd seen God do in prison. I was sure that Phyllis would be happy but skeptical. In the past I hadn't even gone with her to church. Now, I wanted to be a real Christian husband and father to my family. On the plane I rehearsed what I would say.

First, I would tell her of my resolution made that torturous night in the Outhouse, when I promised God that the first Sunday of my return to freedom I would take my family to their home church. At the close of the service I would walk to the front, confess my faith in Christ, and take my responsible place as a member there with my family. In prison I had learned what it means to be isolated, struggling to build my faith alone. I had resolved never to be outside the community of Christian believers again.

Second, I had heard Colonel Flynn in a meditation at Cell 8 in Camp Unity talk about the Scripture, "Let not the sun go down upon your wrath" (Ephesians 4:26). He told how he and his wife Mary Margaret had determined in their marriage never to go to bed before an argument had been settled, the apology made, the angry words forgiven. That brief passage from God's Word really made sense to me, for often I had lain awake at night too proud to say, "I'm sorry," and both of us could feel the hurt.

That first New Year's Eve in Heartbreak Hotel I had resolved never to be without a Bible again. Those verses of God's Word that I had memorized or that I had scrounged from other prisoners' memories had been a living source of strength in my life. I was determined to begin applying God's Word in our family's life together, even in the smallest things.

Third, I can't remember ever praying with Phyllis during our entire married life. In fact, the more involved I got in my career and she in our family, the less we ever really talked with each other, let alone with God. This had to change and change fast. In prison I had worked months trying to get another man "on the line," communicating. Now I had to get my wife and family "on the line" with me. Prayer seemed the perfect way to start. So I resolved to end each day with Phyllis, talking over the day's activities and thanking God for the love we felt from each other and from Him.

Frankly, I was unsure what my wife's reaction to these resolutions might be. I determined on that long flight home to tell her the moment I landed, before we got caught up in the whirl of being together again and before my nervous pride drove me into silence.

On that plane to San Diego, flying across the Pacific Ocean, I practiced every move I would make during our reunion. This wasn't the first time we would be dramatically reunited. Phyllis was a good navy wife. We had spent much of our lifetime waiting to see each other after long tours of duty aboard a carrier or in a foreign base. No matter where I left her, she was always there waiting for me when I returned. When I would walk across the pier or runway to greet her, every reunion was the same. She would come roaring out of the crowd to embrace me in a kind of feet-off-the-ground, full-body tackle.

This time I wanted it to be different. I wanted to hold her at arm's length for one long moment, look into her eyes, tell her that I love her—and then let her tackle me. I had plans, too, for that first moment with my family. During the flight I would ask the stewardess to lend me six napkins. I was going to step off the plane, kiss Phyllis, and then hand each person in my family a napkin to kneel on. Then and there we would thank God for uniting us again. On the runway we would end this drought of prayer in our family once and for all. I had no idea that the television camera would be on us every step of the way, that all my family but Phyllis would await my arrival in the privacy of the beautiful hospital suite, or that there we would say our prayer of thanks together!

We fastened our seat belts for our final descent. The wheels touched the runway. There was a band playing, and cameras were everywhere. It seems like yesterday. I walked down the steps, saluted Admiral Joe Williams and the colors, and heard the crowd's welcome-home applause. Then out of the crowd she ran and planted her own full-body tackle on me. Her feet left the ground and almost knocked me over. All my plans to hold her at arm's length for one long moment, to tell her that I loved her, were forgotten. Thank God! Things were back to normal for the Rutledge family, but they would *never* be the same.

19

REUNION

Phyllis Rutledge
San Diego, California
February 16, 1973

The day Howard was due home in San Diego, the doorbell rang, and a deliveryman handed me a beautiful orchid. It was from my husband. Not since high school had he sent me orchids. Then the government limousine arrived to take us down to Miramar.

It was a dreary, rainy day. I wondered on that short drive to the airport why the sun wasn't shining and the birds singing for Howard's return. The weather got worse as we approached the airport. Imagine San Diego with hail so heavy that it left the golf course looking as if it were covered with snow!

When we arrived at the operations building at Miramar there were TV and radio reporters, cameras, microphones, and mobs of excited people. The plane was due any minute. We were told to wait for our husbands in our limousine, but when I saw another wife standing on the field, I jumped out and ran across the VIP area to get a closer look. Other wives saw me and followed. Suddenly, the sun broke through the clouds, and the silver plane bearing my husband landed and taxied to the waiting crowd. One by one the men got down, and then, as if in a dream, he was standing there. How often I had seen him across crowded waiting rooms, piers, and runways! How often my heart had skipped a beat as he smiled and held out his arms in greeting. But he had been gone so long. Would he smile? Would he hold out his arms again?

Then I heard his name. "Captain Howard Rutledge!" I waited. He saluted Admiral Williams, greeted the press, looked into the crowd. Our eyes met. He smiled and held out his arms. I ran and felt his embrace, my heart crying out its thanks to the God who brought us back together again.

CHARLES L. ALLEN

Life
More
Abundant

GUIDEPOSTS ASSOCIATES, INC.

Carmel, New York

One who lives "Life More Abundant" is
WILBUR H. DAVIES,
a sincere Christian—a great publisher—a
valued friend. With appreciation and affection
I dedicate this book to him.

The Ministry of Books

PEOPLE SMILE when I say, "I have been preaching and I have been married ever since I can remember." That is not literally true, but it comes close. I married the only girl with whom I have ever been in love. We "decided," when we were in first year college, and we married four years later. Marriage has been a wonderful experience for me.

Preaching has also been a wonderful experience, and it is literally true that I have been preaching ever since I can remember. As a little boy—four and five years old —I remember listening to my father preach. I wanted to be a preacher as he was. I recall vividly how that little boy used to slip into the church when nobody was there, put a chair behind the pulpit, stand up in it and preach to the empty pews.

When I was nineteen years old I was assigned as a pastor and, through the years, preaching has been a great joy to me. I thank God for every opportunity He has given me. I am now pastor of a church with nine thousand members, located in the heart of a great city. For nearly twenty years my sermons have been televised to countless thousands of people. I have written regularly in metropolitan newspapers, *The Atlanta Constitution,*

The Houston Chronicle and others, which is a very rewarding ministry. I have had more opportunities than I can count to preach in churches and to large conventions across the country.

But I have come to the conclusion that my greatest opportunity to preach the gospel of Christ has been through the ministry of books. Every day I receive a handful of letters from people who have found something in one of my books, which, they say, has been of help. My publishers tell me that many more than a million people have bought my books, and that is an impressively large congregation.

In this little volume, I have tried to say that the religion of Christ does not take away from life, but adds to the living of each day. Some people just exist, but He came to bring us *Life More Abundant.*

Mrs. Janet Kivett, my secretary, has been very helpful in preparing this manuscript. To her I express deep appreciation.

Charles L. Allen

First Methodist Church
Houston, Texas

Contents

	The Ministry of Books	7
1.	WHY I BELIEVE IN GOD	13
2.	TO BELIEVE IN YOURSELF	20
3.	BE WILLING TO BE YOURSELF	26
4.	HOW TO OVERCOME AN INFERIORITY COMPLEX	32
5.	VICTIMS OF THE OBSTACLE COMPLEX	38
6.	WAITING FOR OUR PROMISED LAND	44
7.	THERE IS A DIFFERENCE BETWEEN YOU AND YOUR ACTIONS	50
8.	THE KEY TO UNLOCK YOURSELF	55
9.	THE FAITH YOU KEEP WILL KEEP YOU	61
10.	FAITH IS THE POWER TO HEAL	67
11.	MIRACLE DRUGS FOR THE SOUL	74
12.	PENICILLIN FOR DESPAIR	79
13.	DON'T LET YOUR DEFEATS DEFEAT YOU	84
14.	POWER TO DESTROY THE EVIL WITH WHICH YOU LIVE	90
15.	CHANGE YOUR THOUGHTS AND YOU CHANGE YOURSELF	96
16.	THE MAGIC OF BELIEVING	102
17.	LOOK AT SOMETHING BIG	109

18.	JESUS' FORMULA FOR PEACE OF MIND	114
19.	THE PEACE HE GIVES	120
20.	WHAT CAN I BELIEVE ABOUT LUCK?	126
21.	WHEN OPPORTUNITY KNOCKS	
	FOR THE LAST TIME	132
22.	WHY AND HOW TO READ THE BIBLE	137
23.	GO DOWN DEATH	143
24.	ETERNAL LIFE	149
25.	WHAT THE BIBLE SAYS ABOUT HEAVEN	155

I.

WHY I BELIEVE IN GOD

WHEN SOMEONE asked me to preach on, "Why I Believe in God," I thought it would be easy to do. Quickly I can think of a dozen reasons to believe in God, but as I look at those reasons I know they are not my reasons. My books on theology give the arguments for God and studying those books has strengthened my faith and confirmed my beliefs. But it would not be honest for me to copy the reasons for belief in God from my books and give them as my own.

The fact is, I believed in God before I ever studied theology. The more I think about it, the more I realize I believed before I knew the reasons. I know now that it is necessary for me to breathe and that without air I would die. But long before I knew that, I just breathed.

I was born into a home where prayer was heard regularly. I did not question that there was a God to hear those prayers. I just accepted the fact. I was taken to church, and it has always seemed normal and right for me to belong to the church. Long before I knew how the church came to be, or the reasons for its existence, I felt at home in it. I am a Christian, and day by day, as I learn more about Christ, I love Him more and I praise Him more for the salvation of my soul. But I do not know when I became a Christian. For years, I have given my life to the ministry and I am sure that is what I should do. But I do not remember when I decided for the ministry. I never thought of doing anything else. I think God created me for that purpose and put it into my mind at birth.

In an American court of law, a person is presumed innocent until he is proved guilty. So it is with my own belief in God. Instead of saying I will not believe until God's existence is proved, I believed and I will continue to believe, until it is proved that there is no God. Until now, I have never had any cause to doubt the existence of God; thus I have never felt the necessity of trying to prove Him.

The Bible feels no necessity for proving God; it assumes God's existence. The Bible's very first words are: "In the beginning God . . ." and it goes on to give us a progressive revelation of God. Moses teaches us the laws of God; Amos reveals His justice; Hosea shows us His love; the Psalms lead us to communion with Him; Micah tells us of His ethical standards; Christ gives us the full revelation of the Father.

Jesus said to His disciples, "Let not your heart be troubled: ye believe in God . . ." (John 14:1). He did not say, *"If* you believe," or "You *should* believe." He simply said, "Ye believe" and went on to tell of the Father's house and the way to it.

God does not depend on reasons or arguments for our belief in Him. God took care of that in our creation. Call it instinct, insight, intuition, or any other name, we were born believing. As we study and learn, as we live and experience, our belief can be strengthened and enlarged. Or our belief can be perverted and misdirected. Therein lies the danger. The Ten Commandments do not command us to believe, but they do command us to keep God as the first object of our worship.

One does not need to understand God in order to believe in Him. The fact is, we understand very few things that we do. In his book, *Nature of the Physical World,* Dr. Arthur Eddington wrote: "I am standing on the threshold about to enter a room. It is a complicated business. In the first place, I must shove against an atmosphere pressing with a force of fourteen pounds on every square inch of my body. I must make sure of landing on a plank traveling at twenty miles a second round the sun. I must do this while hanging from a round planet, head outward into space." Only a few scientists bother to understand what is involved in the process of walking into a room. The rest of us just walk in.

Most of us do not understand the composition of water, but we drink it. None of us know what electricity is, but we use it. Who can understand the process of love? Yet many have given their lives in sacrifice because they loved. Though we cannot explain God, most of us say with Christopher Morley: "I had a thousand questions to ask God; but when I met Him, they all fled and didn't seem to matter."

To say, "I believe in God," means more than just an intellectual assent to the existence of God. It means to trust in Him and to commit our lives to His will. I know a man who was suffering with severe headaches. He went to the doctor and his case was diagnosed as a tumor on the brain. The man had no way of knowing whether or not the doctor was correct. He had to have faith in him.

Because he had faith in the doctor, the man permitted himself to be put to sleep in a room where none of his family or friends were. He gave his consent for the doctor to open his head and cut into his brain. One slip of the knife, one tiny fraction of an inch would have meant instant death to the patient, yet he was willing to have the operation. His belief in the doctor meant he was willing and ready to trust himself to the doctor's hands.

We trust in God because we realize our own weaknesses and inadequacies. As long as we feel sufficient unto ourselves, we do not need God; we are our own God. No person ever really finds God until there is a felt need in his life that only God can fill. Until you need Him, you won't have Him.

We sometimes say it is our duty to go to church, and it is; but very few go for that reason. I would prefer that no one come to my church just from a sense of duty. The ones who gain the most from the church are those who come from a sense of need. Their minds are open to the truth of God, and their hearts are open to the presence of God. The person who comes to church really seeking God will be impressed by the very existence of the church building.

During the singing of the hymns at church, I see many people who inspire me. They have problems and burdens, but they have something else, which enables them to sing. During the time of prayer, I am impressed with the fact that so many do really pray. Surely there must be something to it.

A young lady talked to me about a job in the church. I asked her what salary she expected, and she told me that salary did not matter. She said, "I will live on whatever I get. What I want is the opportunity to serve God." She inspired me, as does the memory of those, down through the centuries, who made large sacrifices for their faith. As the minister reads from the Bible and talks about it, I realize there must be a reason why the Book outlasts all other books. These and other thoughts inspire my spirit, lift my confidence, and make me surer of God.

On the other hand, if one comes to church without a sense of need, he is likely to have a cynical spirit. He finds fault with the building, he looks at the people around him and criticizes them, he doubts the sincerity of the minister, he thinks the choir is trying to show off. That person came for nothing and he receives nothing— better for him to have stayed at home.

We never really believe in God until we feel the need of Him. As Giles Fletcher put it:

He is a path, if any be misled;
He is a robe, if any naked be;
If any chance to hunger, he is bread;
If any be a bondman, he is free;
If any be but weak, how strong is he!
To dead men, life is he; to sick men, health;
To blind men, sight; and to the needy, wealth;
A pleasure without loss, a treasure without stealth.
—*Excellency of Christ*

Tell Me How to Believe in God

"Please tell me how I can believe in God," a friend requested. This friend went on to say, "You talk about God as if everybody knew Him. But I neither know who He is, where He is, or what He does. As far as I know, I have never had any conscious dealing with God. In your

17

sermons you say, 'Put your life in God's hands and He will carry you through.' That is like saying to one who has never flown a plane, 'Get into that jet and fly it wherever you want to go.' I do not doubt the plane's existence or its ability to carry me, but I do know I cannot fly it. As for God, I am not even sure that He exists, and certainly I do not know how to 'put myself in His hands'."

In seeking a plain and straightforward answer I turned to the ninth chapter of St. Mark and read it carefully. Jesus and three of his disciples went up on the mountain and there had a marvelous experience. Before the eyes of the disciples Jesus' raiment became shining; He was transfigured before them. Then Elijah and Moses suddenly appeared and they talked together. It was so wonderful that Peter suggested they just stay on the mountian.

But Jesus knew there was work to be done in the valley below. God never gives His power to those who will not use it in service. At the foot of the mountain was a father who had brought his epileptic son. Since childhood, the boy had been afflicted. The father had asked the disciples to heal the boy but they could not. Now he asked Jesus.

Jesus said, "If thou canst believe, all things are possible to him that believeth" (Mark 9:23). Let's stop on that word "believe." What do we mean by it? "Believe" is used in at least three different senses. A person says, "I believe in the North Pole." He may not have been there, but he accepts the authority of one who has been there. Another says, "I believe that two times two is four." That is something he can reason out for himself. Thus his belief is based on his own intellect. Another says, "I believe the sunshine is warm." He has been in the sunshine and felt it; thus his belief is based on experience. Maybe he cannot explain why the sunshine is warm, but he knows it is.

There are many who sincerely want to believe in God but find it hard. Faith never comes easy, and the only way it can come is by beginning where we can begin and going on from there. No one believes in all of God. No one can. God is so great and we are so small that we can only believe in a part of Him. A man once said to Jesus, "Lord, I believe; help thou mine unbelief" (Mark 9:24). And in every person there is both belief and unbelief. No person believes completely.

The other day I stood on the beach by the ocean. The water lay before me, as far as I could see. I could feel it, I could taste the salt in it, I could swim in it and be carried by the waves. I believe in the ocean because I have seen it and I have felt it. But I do not know the whole sea. I have not been with Admiral Byrd into the Arctic and Antarctic; I have not been into the tropic ocean where the mighty Amazon pours its floods out so freely.

In the ocean are mountain ranges higher and longer than any man has ever seen. There are canyons in the ocean deeper than the dry earth knows of. There is a lot of land area on the earth, but the sea is eighteen times as large. Any man could spend his entire life studying the sea and know only a small part of it. Although we do not know it all, we can still say with assurance, "I believe in the sea."

I can say I believe in people, yet I base that belief on a very limited acquaintance. My immediate family I know intimately. I have some very close friends, and as I go

19

about I meet what seems to me a lot of people. I have met as many as a thousand people in one week. Yet if all the people I have ever seen face to face were put together, they would represent only a very small part of the billions of people of the world. In the people I do know, however, I have seen love and faith, loyalty and unselfishness, goodness and integrity, to the extent that I do believe in people. I do not have to know every person before I learn to believe.

So I believe in God; He is so great that I can never know Him, yet He is so near that I cannot help but know Him. The Bible tells us ". . . God is love" (I John 4:8). I have loved and I have been loved. I have seen love expressed in many ways. Seeing and feeling love, I have come to believe in it. Believing in love is believing in God—a small part of God, to be sure, but still God.

Each day we can know a little more of God. We can never know all of Him, but instead of worrying about the part of God I do not know, I say, "Lord, I believe; help me to believe more."

2.

TO BELIEVE IN YOURSELF

I HAVE A LETTER from a lady who takes me severely to task. She attended my church service recently, and she was shocked that I did not condemn the people for their sins. She wrote me, "Most of the people there were sinners and I suspect you are a worse sinner than any of them."

Her letter disturbed me, not because of what she said, but because what she said is probably true. As I think about it, however, it seems to me we have had more than enough sermons on the sinfulness of man. Someone has wisely said, "The worst way to improve the world is to condemn it." That applies also to a person.

As Jesus stood before a sinful person one day, He said, "Neither do I condemn thee: go, and sin no more" (John 8:11). He was saying to that person, "No matter what your past has been, I still believe in you." As you read the four Gospels, you are constantly impressed by Christ's belief in people and His willingness to trust them. Over and over again He lifted people to a new sense of self-respect and to belief in themselves.

Jesus said, "If thou canst believe, all things are possible to him that believeth" (Mark 9:23). That truth applies to any person in any situation. The father of American psychology, William James, said: "In any project the one important factor is your belief. Without belief there can be no successful outcome. That is fundamental." Ralph Waldo Emerson put it this way: "Belief is absolutely necessary; no accomplishment, no assistance, no training can compensate for lack of belief."

SEE YOURSELF AS SUCCEEDING

Do you believe in yourself? If your answer is negative, you have a serious handicap to overcome. I assure you, however, you can learn to believe in yourself if you will take the three essential steps. The first one is: *Formulate a mental picture of yourself succeeding.*

There is an old story of an outcast beggar who was sitting across the street from an artist's studio. The artist saw him and quickly began to paint his portrait. When it was finished he called the beggar over to look at it. At first the beggar did not recognize himself. "Who is it?" he kept asking. The artist smiled and said nothing.

The beggar kept looking at the portrait until recognition began to dawn. Hesitantly he asked, "Is it I? Can it be I?" The artist replied, "That is the man I see in you." Then the beggar made a wonderful reply. "If that's the man you see," he said, "that's the man I'll be."

Sooner or later, all of us become the person we see ourselves to be. If you develop creative faith in yourself, eventually your faith will recreate you. If your mind is obsessed by thoughts of insecurity and inadequacy, it is because you have allowed such thoughts to dominate your thinking over a period of time. The only way to overcome those thoughts is by putting into your mind a positive pattern of ideas.

The first step to belief in yourself is to plant in your mind a mental picture of yourself succeeding. To start with, your mind will resist that picture. It takes much less mental effort to picture failure and our minds, like running water, seek the easiest course.

Your mind will seek to block your picture of success by building up obstacles. But over against those obstacles, think of your assets and you will see that you have more for you than against you. As you hold tenaciously to your mental picture of success, eventually your mind will accept it and gradually all your powers will focus on that picture and begin to complete it in your actual life.

> If you think you are beaten, you are;
> If you think you dare not, you don't.
> If you want to win but don't think you can,
> It's almost a cinch you won't.
>
> If you think you'll lose, you're lost;
> For out in the world we find
> Success begins with a fellow's will:
> It's all in the state of mind.
>
> If you think you're outclassed, you are;
> You've got to think high to rise;
> You've got to be sure of yourself before
> You can ever win a prize.
>
> Life's battles don't always go
> To the stronger and faster man;
> But sooner or later the man who wins
> Is the man who thinks he can.
> —*Thinking,* Walter D. Wintle

BE WILLING TO BE YOURSELF

The second step to belief in yourself is: *Be willing to be yourself*. One of the quickest ways to depreciate yourself is to become awestruck by other people and to try to copy them. You can be *you* better than you can be anybody else. In fact, you are the only person you can be, and when you try to be somebody else, you end up frustrated and defeated.

Michelangelo once bought an inferior looking piece of marble, which no one else would buy. Asked why he bought it, he said, "Because there's an angel in there and I must set it free." Then he went to work with hammer and chisel and carved a magnificent statue of an angel.

That story reminds us of the fact that within each of us there is a finer person waiting to be set free. You do not need to be someone else; you have it within you, if you will only let it come out. As you develop your finest self, you develop marvelous self-confidence.

A RIGHT RELATIONSHIP WITH GOD

To believe in yourself you must take three essential steps: first, visualize yourself as succeeding; second, be willing to be yourself; and third, *Get into a right relationship with God.* Consider that third step; it is the most important of the three.

William James had a deep understanding of human nature. He said: "Every sort of energy and endurance, of courage and capacity for handling life's evils, is set free in those who have religious faith." Note what he is saying —you have energy, endurance, courage, and capacity, but religious faith is the key that unlocks these powers within you and sets them to work.

Huxley, the English scientist, said that everywhere in England, deep within the soil, are thousands of seeds of tropical plants. They have lain there dormant for years waiting for just one thing—the proper climate. If the climate of England could be changed into a tropical climate, those seeds would immediately spring up into lush, beautiful foliage.

We remember that when certain Egyptian tombs were opened some years ago, wheat was discovered in them. For four thousand years, that wheat had remained in the dry darkness of those tombs. When it was brought out and planted, it grew and produced a crop. All it needed was to be put into proper relationship with the earth, the air, and the sun.

And when you or I come into right relationship with the Spirit of God, when the warmth of His love begins to surround us and when His power begins to flow into us, the energy, endurance, courage, and capacity that have remained dormant within us begin to rise and take hold of our lives.

A father sat on the front porch of his farm home and watched a truck, driven by his own son, turn over into a ditch. He ran to the scene of the accident and found the boy pinned down under the truck in two feet of water. Although he was a small man, the father lifted that truck and pulled his son to safety. The next day he tried to lift the truck again but he couldn't move it. A doctor explained that in the moment of great need nature sent a terrific shot of adrenaline into the man's system, and he had strength he had never known before.

Almighty God built within us certain spiritual mechanisms, and when we use them rightly we have the ability to accomplish things far beyond our normal abilities. Jesus said, ". . . the kingdom of God is within you" (Luke 17:21) ; and He wants to bring it out. St. Paul discovered this power and he said, "I can do all things through Christ which strengtheneth me" (Philippians 4:13). Repeat those words. Repeat them *now*. Keep on repeating them until they become fixed in your mind, so fixed that doubts and fears are driven out. Also, St. Paul said, "If God be for us, who can be against us" (Romans 8:31). Really, who or what can defeat us when God is within us? Believe in God and you will believe in yourself.

3.

BE WILLING TO BE YOURSELF

THE FIRST STEP toward happiness and success in life is this: Be willing to be yourself. As Robert Louis Stevenson put it, "To be what we are, and to become what we are capable of becoming, is the only end of life." I think the major cause of frustration, failure, and unhappiness is our unwillingness to accept ourselves and be ourselves.

In the first place, not to be willing to be yourself is an insult to God. Consider these two statements from the Bible: "All things were made by him; and without him was not any thing made that was made" (John 1:3). "All things" includes me and you. Jesus said, ". . . as my Father hath sent me, even so send I you" (John 20:21).

Before you were born, you existed in the mind of God. He decided that the world needed you at a certain time —that there is something for you to do that is different from what any other person will do. Everything God made has its own peculiar identity. There are billions of blades of grass, but no two alike. No two snowflakes have ever been identical.

No person who ever existed is exactly like you. Even the print of your little finger is separate and distinct. It should lift you to a new realization of importance to know that of all the billions of people the earth has known, there is only one of you.

A sixth-grade teacher asked her class, "What is here in the world today that was not here fifteen years ago?" She expected them to name new inventions. One little boy held up his hand. "What is it, Johnny, that was not here fifteen years ago?" He replied, "Me." He was right. Something new came into the world when you were born. Something that God planned and wanted.

MY BEST POSSIBLE SELF

Second, when I accept myself as myself, I begin working to become my best possible self. God made some men with mechanical abilities and some with artistic abilities; He made some women beautiful and some homely; He made some people short and others tall. While we can improve and develop, none of us can really change ourselves. Long ago, I accepted the idea that God made me to be a preacher. Also, I accepted the idea that I wasn't made to be a Peter Marshall, a Norman Vincent Peale, or a Ralph Sockman. He made those men to do their work. As much as I may wish it were different, I also accepted the idea that I was made to be

27

Charles Allen. So, the only thing left for me to do is do the best with Charles Allen that I can. That is also true for you.

Willingness to be yourself will rid your life of all jealousy and envy. It will eliminate all feelings of inferiority. It will set you free for the giving of yourself to life as you have opportunity, without fear of failure or defeat. When you really decide to be yourself, you know you can succeed. That is the one thing you can do. When you secretly want to be someone else—that is when you become unhappy and begin to fail.

Every person is really two selves—the self he is and the self he has the possibility of becoming. Highest success will come to you when you begin to picture in your mind your best possible self.

Someone asked Thomas Edison how he accounted for his amazing inventive genius. He replied, "It is because I never think in words, I think in pictures." He pictured in his mind some object he desired to invent. This picture then took possession of him. It sank into his subconscious mind and, even while he was thinking of something else, his subconscious mind worked on it. Because the subconscious mind has marvelous creative power, he got flashes of insight—"creative hunches" he called them—and that accounted for his greatness.

A successful short-story writer told me that he always wrote his stories backwards. First he wrote the ending, and then he wrote the story to fit it. That is a good way to look at your own life. Get in mind the ending, your highest goal, and then you will naturally make your life the story to fit it.

Harold Sherman tells about a miserable, miserly lady

who saved her money, but finally lost everything. She told him, "What I have feared has come. Here I am old and penniless. Now there is nothing for me but the poorhouse." He rebuked her: "There you go again. You thought poverty, you feared poverty, you pictured poverty until it came. Now you want the poorhouse. Keep thinking about it and that is exactly what you will get."

Being a wise counselor, he led her to think positively. She didn't regain her lost wealth, but she did later become employed as a companion to a woman of wealth, and as such she traveled widely and was happier than she had ever been before. Yes, you must be yourself, but be sure to think in terms of your best possible self.

Let me give you a simple plan that works:

(1) Write down exactly what you want. Be specific and clear; don't deal in vague generalities. Keep working on it until you can state your goals in life in a hundred words or less. Be sure that is what you want.

(2) Read in your Bible Mark 11:24. "What things soever ye desire, when ye pray, believe that ye receive them, and ye shall have them." This is not as "magical" as it first sounds. If your desires are unreasonable and not according to the will of God, it will not be possible for you to believe.

(3) Read what you have written aloud to yourself at least twice each day, until it becomes the dominating thought in your mind. Let the picture take complete possession of you, and then you will give yourself completely to that picture.

This may sound simple, but I tell you the results can be amazing.

29

When I was a pastor in Atlanta, the church contracted with a firm in England for twenty-five stained-glass windows, presenting the life of Christ. It was not too difficult to decide on the particular scenes to be used, except in one case.

Which scene from His life should be in the window back of the pulpit? Since that was the window the people would be looking into as they worshiped, we wanted to be sure it was the right one. What would it be? His birth? The Lord preaching, praying? The shepherd? The Last Supper? The cross? His resurrection? Any of those would have been appropriate, but we did not select any of them.

Just before His ascension, He said to His disciples, "Go ye . . . and, lo, I am with you alway . . ." (Matthew 28:19-20). This is the one we decided on for the focal point in the church. Think about it. These disciples had committed so many blunders and they were limited men in so many ways. They had even denied their Lord and had acted in a cowardly and shameful fashion. But in spite of that, Jesus was willing to trust His work into their hands and He promised His Presence and Power to them. Those men never faltered after that. When we believe ourselves to be within the will of God and know He is helping us, we will not fail.

"Lo, I am with you alway." That assurance gives to one a sense of conquering support. Recently, I was talking with a man who gives all of his time to financial campaigns. His company has been doing that work for many years, and they know a lot about it. One rule they insist on is that solicitors go out in pairs. After much experience, they have learned that two solicitors working together will raise four times as much money as one going alone.

Jesus understood that principle, and when He sent His disciples out, you remember, the Bible tells us, "And he called unto him the twelve, and began to send them forth by two and two" (Mark 6:7). There is strength in companionship. Just before Christ ascended, He gave them the assurance that He would be with them. They believed and did not doubt, and because of His Presence, they became conquerors of the world.

The realization of His Presence gives us guidance. A man gave me this testimony: He was in serious difficulty. He thought about what he should do, but everything he tried seemed to fail. One day he asked himself, "What would Christ do?" He asked that question honestly. That is, in asking he was also committing himself to the answer, whatever it might be. He found the answer, and now that question has become the habit of his life.

"What would Christ do?" When we accept for ourselves the answer to that question, our shoulders straighten up, our eyes light up, power overcomes our weakness, and victory drives away our defeat. We look life straight in the eye as we say, "I can do all things through Christ which strengtheneth me" (Philippians 4:13).

4.

HOW TO OVERCOME
AN INFERIORITY COMPLEX

"HOW TO OVERCOME an Inferiority Complex." That is something nearly every person would like to know. Most of us have moments when we feel defeated and inadequate. We often feel inferior as we face the circumstances of our lives.

In the hospital the other day, a man I was visiting said to me, "It's no use. This thing is bigger than I am and I can't handle it." His doctor says he could make a complete recovery if he could only begin to believe in himself. But he has accepted the idea of defeat and has surrendered to it. It is much easier to surrender to an inferiority complex than to overcome it, and a lot of people have done just that.

But to those who really want to gain confidence and power, who are unwilling to give up and quit, I can show the path to follow. You will find it in the seventeenth chapter of I Samuel. There were two armies at war. One was encamped on a mountain on one side of a valley; the other was on a mountain on the opposite side. At that time there was a lull in the fighting.

One morning there came out of the Philistines' camp a

man by the name of Goliath. He was a tremendous man, whose height was six cubits and a span. He wore a helmet of brass, a coat of iron, and heavy coverings on his legs. In one hand he carried a long spear, and in the other hand an enormous shield. He was a fearful-looking fellow. In fact, he was a giant.

He cried out to the armies of Israel, challenging them to select a man to come forward and do battle. The story says, "When Saul and all Israel heard those words of the Philistine, they were dismayed, and greatly afraid" (17:11). Goliath gave that entire army an inferiority complex. Notice again those words, ". . . they were dismayed, and greatly afraid." You couldn't describe the effects of an inferiority complex better if you wrote a book about it.

In the army of Israel were several sons of Jesse. The father was concerned about his sons so one day he sent David, the youngest, to carry some extra food to his brothers. Also, he was to see how the boys were getting along. To visit the camp of the army must have been a thrilling mission for young David. He found his brothers and, as they were talking, big Goliath came out and issued his challenge to fight. David saw how the men "fled from him, and were sore afraid" (17:24).

So David went to Saul and volunteered to fight Goliath. Saul laughed and said, ". . . thou art but a youth. . . ." Then David told the King how he had slain both a lion and a bear that had come to attack his sheep. He told the King how God had given him strength in those fights. And now he had reason to believe that God would help him in his fight against Goliath.

The King was persuaded by the courageous confidence

of young David and gave his permission. Down the mountain and across the valley toward Goliath David marched.

WE ALL FACE GIANTS

David is not the last person to be confronted by a giant. In fact, we all have our giants and that is why so many people develop inferiority complexes. If there were no giants, you would not feel inferior.

We remember how the children of Israel came to the border of their Promised Land. They appointed a committee to spy out the land. They found it to be a good land, "flowing with milk and honey," and they so much wanted to possess it. The majority reported, however, "there we saw giants, and we were in our own sight as grasshoppers" (Numbers 13:33).

Some of the giants in our lives are real. Others are imaginary. But whether they are real or not, the trouble comes when we allow the giants to make us as grasshoppers, "dismayed and afraid"; when, instead of giving our best, we give up and quit. Your giant may be some physical handicap; it may be a hard job that is before you; it may be a deep sorrow, a financial debt, a feeling of loneliness, a harmful habit, or one of many things. David did not minimize the strength of the giant, but neither did he let the giant minimize him. The first step in overcoming an inferiority complex is to consider your own strength and power, as well as the strength of the adversary in your life.

The second step is to go forth and do battle with the giant. You will never win a fight if you don't fight. Before David went forth to battle, he decided how best he could do it. Saul took off his own armor and put it on David. I can see in my mind this boy wearing Saul's brass helmet and coat of iron. Then he took Saul's sword in his hand. But Saul's armor didn't fit David. More than that, this shepherd boy did not know how to use that big sword. So he took off the armor and handed it back.

That was the wisest thing David could have done. He realized that he had to fight the giant in his own way. So he took a sling out of his pocket, gathered up five stones and went forth. There is a great lesson to learn. One reason many people have an inferiority complex is that they try to be somebody else instead of just themselves. If God had wanted you to be like someone else, He would have made you like that. Instead, He made you as you are and He expects you to be yourself.

When I started out to preach, I felt that I wanted to be like my father. I still would like to be as he was. I have every sermon he ever wrote, but I have never used one of them. I would if I could because they are better than my sermons, but I don't have his personality; and if I tried to use his sermons, I would fail completely. Instead, I must use my own personality and write my own sermons and have confidence in my own way of doing things.

Suppose David had said, "All I have is a sling, so I can't fight." He would have failed miserably. The secret of success is to determine what you have and then have the courage and energy to use it.

When David went out to meet Goliath, it seemed to be a hopeless fight for him, a young shepherd boy facing a mighty giant trained in the art of warfare. In addition, the giant was fully armed while David had only a sling and some small stones. The Bible says Goliath "disdained him," cursed him and vowed to feed his flesh to the fowls of the air and the beasts of the field.

David was not afraid, however. Very calmly he replied to the giant, and his reply is one of the most sublime expressions of faith in the entire Bible. He said, "Thou comest to me with a sword, and with a spear, and with a shield: but I come to thee in the name of the Lord of hosts . . ." (I Samuel 17:45).

Carefully David placed the stone in his sling. He began to whirl it around his head; he took aim and let it go. That stone found its mark on the giant's forehead. He fell on his face. David had five stones, but he needed only one. If we use what we have, it is generally true that we have more than we actually need to win the victory.

Then David went over and put his foot on the fallen giant, took the giant's own sword, and cut off his head at the shoulders. That was pretty drastic but it was the custom in those days. When the Philistines saw what had happened, they took to their heels. The army of Israel gained courage from David, and they took out after them and routed them. And Saul, when he saw what had happened, made David his assistant. Later David became the king.

It is a great story. It has meaning for the twentieth century. We may read a hundred books on psychology, but we won't find a better way of overcoming an inferiority complex.

The Saturday afternoon before I was to preach my first sermon as pastor of Grace Church in Atlanta, I was in the church alone. It seemed so big and strange to me that I was almost paralyzed by fear. I was much younger then and I knew nothing about a big city church. I knew I would fail miserably. Then I walked down the aisle and knelt at the altar and prayed. I felt a calm spirit coming over me, and I left the church that day with joy and peace in my heart.

At the close of my sermon the next night, I told of my experience and gave opportunity to those present to come and pray at the altar. I repeated that invitation every Sunday night for the twelve years I was pastor of that church. Thousands did as I did and went out of the church to face the tasks of the coming week with confidence and without fear.

When one stands at his full height in the face of obstacles, when one refuses to shrink back but instead gives his own best, when one sincerely says to life, "I come to you in the name of the Lord," the inhibitions are taken away, the tangles are cleared, and the clouds of life are lifted.

5.

VICTIMS OF
THE OBSTACLE COMPLEX

VAST NUMBERS of people are victims of the obstacle complex. These people have become convinced that certain difficulties or circumstances stand in their way and that it is impossible for them to reach the goals in life they most want. Let me illustrate with one of the classic examples of history.

The children of Israel were in bondage in Egypt, but God had put into their minds the vision of a better life. He had promised them a land—a land in which they would have all that they wanted. During their hard labor and extreme want, they were sustained by the hope of their Promised Land. Finally the day came when their dreams began to come true.

At least they made a start. Under the leadership of Moses, they threw off the bondage of Pharaoh and moved out of Egypt. It was a long and painful journey of forty years, but along the way they had many evidences of the power of God. He divided the Red Sea and brought them safely out on the other side; He guided them through the wilderness with a pillar of cloud by day and of fire by night. He provided food day by day.

Finally, they reached the very border of their Promised Land. There they stopped to ask questions. That was their first mistake. They began to ask, "Can we possess the land?" God had promised it to them; again and again, He had proved His power and His willingness to help them, but now they hesitated. For nine generations, they had been in bondage; for forty years, they had struggled across the wilderness—why did they hesitate on the border? They had everything to gain and nothing to lose, but still they hesitated.

Shakespeare was right when he said:

> There is a tide in the affairs of men
> Which, taken at the flood, leads on to fortune;
> Omitted, all the voyage of their life
> Is bound in shallows and in miseries.
> —*Julius Caesar*, Act IV, Scene 3

They appointed a committee of twelve to spy out the land. The committee reported it was a good land, "flowing with milk and honey." Caleb spoke up and said, "Let us go up at once, and possess it; for we are well able to overcome it." But others on the committee said, "We be not able to go up against the people; for they are stronger than we. . . . And there we saw the giants . . . and we were in our own sight as grasshoppers . . ." (Numbers 13:30-33).

It is a lot easier to surrender to giants than it is to fight them, so they stopped. They became victims of the obstacle complex. They murdered their opportunity; they lost their chance.

That isn't an old story. It is as new as today's newspaper. We dream of being something better. We believe God wants us to have the more abundant life. We have every assurance of His help. But we see obstacles in the way and we become shrinking cowards, saying, "I can't," "It's impossible," "It isn't for me"; and we hesitate; we stop; we lose out.

Remember: success comes in *cans,* failure in *can'ts.* So, get hold of a *can*-opener and start using it.

Whoever you are, there are three basic facts that you can depend on. First, God has for you a "promised land." Second, there will be difficulties in your way. Third, with your own ability and God's help, you can be the person God intends and reach the goals in life that God has shown you through your hopes and dreams.

In truth, each one of us is standing, right at this moment, at the exact spot on which the children of Israel once stood, on the very border of our promised land. But it is also true that vast numbers never really possess their land. They end up frustrated, defeated, and miserable. Why do people fail to reach the top of their abilities in life? There are three reasons:

We Concentrate on Obstacles Instead of Strengths

First, they concentrate on the obstacles in their way instead of on their strengths. "We saw giants standing between us and our Promised Land," the children of Israel said. And we say the same thing. The fact is that every person has had obstacles to overcome.

Whenever I get discouraged, I like to think about some of the great names in history and the giants they faced. Sir Walter Scott limped through life on club feet. Napoleon was an epileptic. John Milton, who wrote *Paradise Lost,* was blind, as was Homer, the great Greek poet.

Louisa May Alcott, who wrote *Little Women,* a book that has been read by millions, was told by an editor that she had no writing ability and advised to stick to her sewing. When Walt Disney submitted his first drawings for publication, the editor told him he had no talent. The teachers of Thomas A. Edison said he was too stupid to learn. F. W. Woolworth built a great chain of stores, but when he was twenty-one years old he was not permitted to wait on the customers in the store where he worked. His employers said he did not have sense enough to meet the public. Josiah Wedgwood, whose name stands for lovely china, was a lame, uneducated, neglected boy. Beethoven was deaf. Before Admiral Richard E. Byrd flew over the North Pole and the South Pole, he was retired from the United States Navy as unfit for service.

But we say, "Others could overcome their obstacles, but my case is different." The only difference is that some people fight to overcome their obstacles, while others sit back and let their obstacles overcome them. Some people live on top of the world; others live with the world on top of them.

"We saw giants—we are as grasshoppers," said the children of Israel. Remember this fact: If you concentrate on your obstacles, they will grow into giants and you will sink into a grasshopper. But if you concentrate on your powers, you will become the giant and your obstacles will become like grasshoppers. It depends on which view you decide to take.

A second reason why we fail to possess our individual life's promised land is that we are not willing to pay the price.

There is a wonderful life within reach of every person—our promised land. God put it into our dreams; He gave us the ability to hope. But promised lands never come cheaply.

A boy told me the other day he had to give up his hopes of a college education because he didn't have enough money. I thought back to the days when I was in college. I remember a boy who made his way through college by milking twenty cows every morning before breakfast and every afternoon before supper. Another one got up every morning at three o'clock and worked four hours as a night watchman. I thought of many I know today who work all day and then go to school at night.

Too many young people today, when they look for a job, are only concerned about two things—the number of hours and the amount of the salary. But a few people forget hours and think of opportunity.

God has a promised land for you, but it remains for you to say with Caleb of old, "Let us go up at once, and possess it; for we are well able to overcome it" (Numbers 13:30). Caleb believed in himself, and he was willing to fight the battles, but he had still a third thing: He had faith in God.

If there is some obstacle blocking the pathway to your promised land, whether it be lack of opportunity, some opposition, or some personal weakness, read again Jesus' words in Matthew 17:20: "If ye have faith as a grain of mustard seed, ye shall say unto this mountain, Remove hence to yonder place; and it shall remove; and nothing shall be impossible unto you."

There is hardly anything smaller than a mustard seed, and there is hardly anything larger than a mountain. And through the use of those two illustrations, Jesus is saying a little faith can have large consequences. When you face a mountain of fear, or of handicaps, or of difficulties in your home life, or of an unhappy job, or of monthly bills—remember the Lord said, faith moves mountains.

And how does one go about getting faith? I quoted Jesus' statement about faith and mountains. He said it to a group of people who had failed at a task. Then in the very next verse He said, ". . . this kind goeth not out but by prayer. . . ." Prayer is the food of faith. Why is that so? Because prayer is the doorway into the Presence of God.

Before a great battle, Napoleon would stand alone in his tent and one by one his marshals would enter, grasp his hand in silence and go out again. In his book, *Learning to Have Faith,* Dr. John A. Redhead has this wonderful line: "Power comes from the Presence, and the way to power is the practice of the Presence."

Tonight when you say your prayers, take your mind off your obstacles and think of God. Say, "I can do all things through Christ which strengtheneth me" (Philippians 4:13). Keep saying it over and over until you get the feel of it. Say, "If God be for us, who can be against us" (Romans 8:31). Say it so many times that it begins to take possession of you. And as you possess faith and become possessed by faith, you will at the same time begin to possess your promised land.

6.

WAITING FOR
OUR PROMISED LAND

FOR GENERATIONS the children of Israel were slaves in Egypt. They were forced to do the most menial work and live under the most humiliating circumstances. It was hard for them to bear that bondage.

They were a proud people, descendants of the greatest men of history. In their veins flowed noble blood. In them was the stuff of poets and prophets. Making brick as slaves was unnatural for those people. How they must have resented being in Egypt! But they were sustained by a promise of God, His promise of a land of their own where they could follow the way of life they were created for. They lived on hope—hope based on their belief in the faithfulness of God.

But for nine generations they were kept in slavery. Surely they grew weary in waiting. Why were they held back so long? Perhaps God was waiting for a Moses to rise up. Maybe God had to wait until the people were ready to follow His leadership. Even after they left Egypt, they were forced to wander forty long years in the wilderness. But during those forty years they were in training, developing their laws and their power to govern themselves.

Even at the border of the Promised Land, they had to wait—to wait until they were willing to pay the price to possess their land. It was Mohammed who said, "Whatever God hath ordained, can only be attained by striving." They saw giants in their Promised Land, and they shrank from fighting them. Promised lands never come cheaply. There are always difficulties in the way of possessing them. But finally the children of Israel did come into their own Promised Land.

JESUS HAD TO WAIT

That story is about a group of people, but it is just as true for the individual person. Look at the most thrilling example of all time, the story of Christ. He said, ". . . I must be about my Father's business . . ." (Luke 2:49) ; "I came . . . not to do mine own will, but the will of him that sent me" (John 6:38) ; ". . . he that hath sent me is with me" (John 8:29).

As some poet has said:

> Jesus, too, had a Promised Land,
> But it wasn't a place,
> It was a plan.

A plan for His life, a work to be done, a place to be

filled; God's plan for Christ was the establishment of a kingdom—the Kingdom of God. It meant the creating on earth of a society in which love, peace, and righteousness would reign. It was a thrilling and glorious way to spend one's life.

Yet Jesus, too, had to wait in some land of bondage. His Egypt was a carpenter's shop. Circumstance was the pharaoh that held Him in captivity. No doubt Joseph had died when Jesus was a teen-age boy. On His shoulders fell the responsibility of earning a living for Himself and Mary and his smaller brothers and sisters. No doubt His ambition was to go to college, but He forever lost that chance. Circumstances stood in the way of His dreams and brought disappointment instead of fulfillment.

Jesus had to wait, and wait, and wait to get out of bondage and to journey toward His promised land. But maybe the waiting was part of God's plan for His Son.

Within the breast of Christ was burning a fire. It was the consciousness of God's plan for His life. Surely He was anxious to get started, to see results, to achieve His life's purpose. But circumstances held Him in slavery.

Instead of preaching the good news of the Kingdom, He was forced to saw planks and hammer nails. It was such menial work for the Son of God to be doing. It caused Him to miss going to college. Every day He was held back, it seemed, was a day lost. But the days went into months and into years, and still He had to wait. His chance did not come until He was thirty years old. In those days, thirty years old was approaching old age.

But as you study His entire life, you begin to feel that the waiting was part of God's plan. Certainly Jesus used His circumstances in the finest possible way. Instead of becoming bitter, instead of surrendering His dreams, in-

46

stead of turning to some lesser purpose, He held fast to His promised land and at the same time was faithful to life, day by day. As we study His later ministry, we see that the opportunities of His limited "today" became the stones out of which He built His castle tomorrow.

He became trained and conditioned in the school of experience, instead of in college. I don't know what the scholars might have taught Him, but we do know many of the things He learned day by day, and we know how He used His knowledge for the glory of God.

Someone imagines that one day a farmer came to him for estimates on the building of a new barn. While at Jesus' shop, the farmer boasted loudly of his great abundance and talked profanely about the kind of life he lived. But the next week that farmer's son came to Jesus to get a coffin made in which to bury his father. As Jesus made the coffin, He thought about that man and the mistakes he had made. Later Jesus was not in the carpenter's shop; instead He was preaching to the multitudes. He saw in them a mad desire for things. He remembered that farmer of past years and He told them the story (Luke 12:16-21). It was a story they could understand, and by the use of that experience, Jesus taught the truth of God.

So it was with all of those matchless stories He told. They came out of life, His own life, and they had great meaning for the people. In the school of experience Jesus learned well the lessons of life, and as a result, the Bible says, ". . . the common people heard him gladly" (Mark 12:37). Being able to win the common people, helped Him gain the followers who would carry on His work.

In many instances the handicaps, frustrations, and disappointments of life hold us in bondage and away

47

from the realization of our highest purposes. Yet it is also true that as we are faithful day by day, the life circumstances we are forced to live with prepare us for the possession of our own personal promised land.

We Have to Wait, too

We believe God has a plan for each of our lives. But just as the children of Israel were held back from the Promised Land by their bondage in Egypt, and just as Jesus was delayed so long in His mission by the circumstances that forced Him to work in a carpenter's shop, so do we sometimes feel enslaved by the circumstances and frustrations of life.

One day Moses came to lead the children of Israel out of bondage, and one day Jesus closed the door of His shop for the last time and went forth preaching. But the question for many people is, "Will the moment of release ever come for me?"

First, let me say, as Browning said, in *Pippa Passes,* "All service ranks the same with God." It is not the work we do, but the spirit within us that determines our real lives. If work is done in the spirit of consecration, it is just as sacred to sell soap as it is to preach sermons, or to be a butcher as it is to be a bishop. Your present work can be done for the glory of God—but there is something more to be said.

Second, for every person who is faithful to the living of each day, there will come an hour of destiny—a time of self-fulfillment. It will come, I emphasize, if we remain faithful to the daily tasks without losing heart or hope. No member of God's team trains for the race without one day being given a chance to run. Sooner or later God says to every person who is ready, "Now—now your moment has come."

We remember that Jesus said to His disciples, ". . . as my Father hath sent me, even so send I you" (John 20:21). But to them He also said, ". . . tarry ye in the city of Jerusalem, until ye be endued with power from on high" (Luke 24:49). That is, God will use you when you become consecrated to His will and purposes and possess His Spirit.

Here is an illustration. A great violinist thrilled his audience with his playing. At the end of the selection, he smashed the violin into a hundred pieces over a chair. The people sat aghast. Then he picked up another violin and said, "Don't be alarmed. The one I smashed was purchased for only a few dollars in a shop down the street. I shall now play upon my Stradivarius." He played the same selection but the majority of the people could not tell the difference.

Then the violinist said, "Friends, so much has been said about the value of my violin that I wanted to impress upon you the fact that the music is not in the instrument; it is in the one who plays upon it."

So it is with us. Our talents are varied. Many of us are conscious of our limitations. We are tempted to feel we are too unimportant to matter. But when we put ourselves into God's hands, when His purposes become our purposes, when we pray, ". . . nevertheless not my will, but thine, be done" (Luke 22:42), the great Master of us all will be able to produce through the lives of each of us the great music of life. But He cannot use a life until it is put into His hands.

49

7.

THERE IS A DIFFERENCE BETWEEN YOU AND YOUR ACTIONS

"THOU SHALT LOVE thy neighbour as thyself," said Jesus (Matthew 19:19). Let's take that sentence apart and look at it more closely. "Thou shalt love"—that seems like a contradiction in terms. "Thou shalt" is a command, and a command implies force. An officer in the army issues a command to a soldier. Maybe the soldier does not wish to comply with the command, but he does it anyway. The soldier uses his will power to force himself to obey.

But can love be commanded? Even if it could, who would want to receive someone's commanded love? Sometimes we command our children to turn off the television and study their lessons. They don't want to do it but after some argument, if they decide we really mean what we say, they will obey reluctantly. A child can be made to study, whether he wants to or not. Suppose I say to my children, "I command you to love me". No, we think love must come as a result of something else other than the force of command. Yet Jesus said, "Thou shalt love."

Who does Jesus command us to love? "Thy neighbor,"

He says. Once a man asked the question, "Who is my neighbor?" In reply Jesus told him a story about a Samaritan, a man of another race. If you are a white person and asked Him that question, He might tell you a story about a Negro. If you are a Protestant, He might tell you about a Catholic. If you hold resentment in your heart toward some person, our Lord might make that very person the center of a story telling you who your neighbor is. Ask Jesus, "Who is my neighbor?" He will point to the one you resent the most and say, "There is your neighbor." "Thou shalt love thy neighbor," Jesus said.

"As thyself," our Lord said we should love. Here we have the key that unlocks the door to the meaning of this command to love. Every person loves himself or herself. Self-love is both normal and right. Jesus does not condemn our love. In fact, the clear implication of His command commends and upholds self-love. Yet self-love does not always mean self-approval. In one of his poems, Edgar A. Guest says:

> I don't want to stand with the setting sun
> And hate myself for the things I've done.

DISTINCTION BETWEEN SELF AND ACTIONS

We don't ever really hate ourselves, but very often we do hate the things we have done. Sometimes our actions are stupid; sometimes they are selfish; sometimes they are bad tempered. In looking back at such actions, we feel shame, regret, and even hate. We despise the

51

thing we have done or said, yet at the same time we continue to love ourselves. You see, we make a distinction between ourselves and our actions.

Certainly we allow that distinction in reference to our own selves. We do something that is not right and that is beneath our standards, and we say, "That was not the real me." "I am ashamed of what I did," we say.

Will Rogers used to say, "I have never met a man I did not like." That statement needs interpretation. Most of us meet a person we don't like every time we look in the mirror. That is, we have weaknesses that we don't like and wish we were rid of. We remember things we have said and done that we don't like and wish we could change.

Even in the best friend you have, you see some things you don't like. Some people's faults are so offensive to you that you feel you thoroughly dislike that person. When you look more closely, however, you realize it is the person's actions rather than the person that you dislike. We recall how Jesus said of the Prodigal Son, "And when he came to himself . . ." (Luke 15:17).

That boy was thoroughly selfish and he lived in a selfish spirit. Nobody likes that. But when we realize it was not the real person who was acting that way, we forgive his actions and we love him in spite of what he did. When Jesus commands, "Love thy neighbour as thyself," He doesn't mean that we must like everything someone else does. He does mean we must not hold hatred or ill will in our hearts against the real person. It means more—because love is an active force rather than just an emotional feeling. To love means to give ourselves in every possible opportunity of service. The emotion of love cannot be commanded, but service of love can be. And if the service of love is sincere, eventually we will feel the emotion of love.

Let me use the finest illustration the world has ever seen. It is Christ on the cross. Certainly He did not like the actions of certain people that day. They were cruel and crude; they were heartless and very unfair. Christ could never like such actions. Yet He looked beyond their actions and He saw them. While He hated the sin, He loved the sinner. Since love always expresses itself in the best way that it can under the circumstances, Christ did something even for those who were crucifying Him. He prayed for the forgiveness of their sins. He always expressed His love.

When a leper came, though He did not like leprosy, He healed and blessed the man. To a paralytic He said, "Thy sins be forgiven." When He saw Zacchaeus, certainly He did not like the theiving trickery of the man, yet He took time to help him find the better way. Christ said ". . . he that hath seen me hath seen the Father . . ." (John 14:9). Sometimes I look at certain people and I wonder how even God could love them. Then I think of myself, and with even greater wonder do I realize He loves me. Remembering His love for me helps me to obey His command to love my fellowman, no matter what he may have done.

A Lady Who Forgave

When I was preaching in a series of services in Florida, a lady phoned asking to see me. She seemed in distress, but I could not possibly free any time for her until after the service that night. I promised to talk with her then. When I did meet her, she was smiling and so happy she seemed to bubble over.

I asked, "Are you sure you're the lady who phoned me this morning?" She said, "Yes, but I don't need your help now, so I won't keep you." I said, "When a person has changed as completely as you have, I want to know what happened." So we sat down on the front pew of the church and she told me her story.

Her husband died suddenly, leaving no money or insurance for the support of their four children and herself. He did have, however, a small electrical supply business. In the business was a man her husband had trained for six years. She felt she could carry on the business with that man's help.

She had one competitor in the community and that man tried to buy her out, offering only a fraction of what her business was worth. When she wouldn't sell, he became angry and told her he would force her out. He cut prices and did everything he could against her, yet she held on. Then one day, the man her husband had trained told her he was quitting. He was going to work for the other man, who had offered him more salary than she could pay.

She carried on by herself as best she could, but it was a struggle. Sometimes her children did not have enough to eat. Worse was the hatred she had in her heart against that man. Hate is poison both for our souls and our bodies, and she knew that. Yet she could not seem to do anything about it. It was in such a situation she had phoned me that morning. That night, she arranged for a neighbor to sit with her children and she came to church to talk with me about it after the service.

My sermon that night was on the cross. I told about

how through the power of mental television—imagination and memory—we can actually see back across the years. In detail, I described how He prayed in Gethsemane, the coming of the soldiers, the betraying kiss of one He had trusted, His trials before Herod and Pilate. I told about His humiliation before that mob as they stripped off His clothes, how they drove the nails, hung Him up to die, and then spit on Him, mocked and ridiculed.

I took about forty-five minutes to describe that picture as vividly as I could. Then I said, "Listen! He is about to speak!" We strained our ears, and across the centuries His voice came clear and strong, saying, "Father, forgive them." Then I invited those present to come to the altar and pray.

This woman told me that as she knelt, the only thing she could think of was the man she hated. She found herself praying for him. She prayed the prayer the Master prayed. She felt cleansed and whole again. She told me that now she had no fear of the future. When Christ comes into our hearts, we can love even as He loved.

8.
THE KEY TO UNLOCK YOURSELF

THERE IS A POOR fellow in the Bible who has my sympathy. He was given a talent, which represented ability and opportunity. True, he was not given as many talents as some others, but he did have at least one. He could have amounted to something. Instead he explained to his Lord, ". . . I was afraid, and went and hid thy talent in the earth . . ." (Matthew 25:25).

A lot of people today are like that man. They have buried themselves in some prison of hopelessness, despair, and uselessness. "I was afraid," the man said. A physician kept a record over a period of years of the fears of his patients. He found that 40 percent were afraid of things that never happened; 30 percent were afraid because of past events about which they could do nothing; 12 percent were afraid of some imaginary illness; 10 percent were afraid of something that might happen to some loved one. Only 8 percent of the fears had real causes—92 percent of the fears were needless. Yet real or unreal, fear can cause you to become a locked-up person, unhappy and useless.

What is the key that will unlock yourself? Long years ago, the prophet Isaiah was concerned about the future of his people. He assured them that if they would seek God's guidance, they would find it. He said, "And thine ears shall hear a word behind thee, saying, This is the way, walk ye in it . . ." (Isaiah 30:21). Until one hears and obeys that voice, he is never set entirely free.

It is a matter of making up your mind once and for all that you will accept God's will for your life no matter what it is. But before you can hear God's voice, you must make the commitment. God doesn't bargain with us. He expects us to trust Him to the point of absolute surrender. The Prodigal Son didn't say to the father, "Before I decide to come back home, I want to know what you will expect of me." Instead, he came saying, ". . . make me as one of thy hired servants" (Luke 15:19).

Make me—make me—make me. He surrendered to the father's will.

You Begin to Walk

When you decide God's way shall be your way, immediately you begin to walk. You stop worrying about whether you will fail or not; you just launch out on faith. There is a story of a young bear cub who was puzzled about how to walk. The little bear said to its mother, "Shall I move my right foot first, or my left, or my two front feet together, or the ones on the left side together and then the ones on the right side?" The mother bear said, "Leave off thinking about it and just walk."

We think about this problem and that one, about the future and where it might lead, and we get so confused we don't know which way to move. But when we say with Christ, "Thy will be done," we do see at least the first step and we find the strength to take that step. At this very moment say with me, "Now I yield my life to God's will, whatever His will may be." That is surrender, but surrender based on high faith and surrender that leads to complete victory.

You Turn From the Unhappy Past

Complete yielding to the will of God is the key that will open the tomb of your buried self and set you to really living. That commitment will take all the fears out of your life, because it turns your face away from your unhappy past and causes you to face the future with anticipation instead of apprehension.

The realization of being within God's will immediately rids your mind of any thought of failure. I refer frequently to the experiment the Coués used many years ago. They would place a plank twelve inches wide on the ground and invite people to walk it. Anyone could walk that. Then they would place that same plank on supports high in the air and ask the same people to walk it. Only a few would dare try. Most of the others would have failed, if they had tried.

The point is easily seen. With the plank on the ground one thinks only of walking it. But with the plank high in the air, one thinks of falling. And it is a well-attested fact of life that what we think is usually what will happen. When we give ourselves to God's will, the center of our attention is not ourselves and our weaknesses, but God and His strength. And one who has faith in God cannot think of Him as failing or of being defeated.

Faith gives to one a courageous heart. I was riding with a man the other day in a new car he had just bought. He explained the fine features of the car, and he seemed especially proud of its power. "In fact," he said, "it has an extra, hidden power." Then the car seemed to just leap forward. So sudden was the speed that it threw me back against the seat. He explained that when you press the accelerator against the floor, the motor shifts into the power gear and gives that extra burst of speed.

I thought, that is what happens when a person takes God into his life. He goes along under his normal power, but he knows there is still a greater Power within reach, ready to give him an extra push when it is needed.

We remember that the Psalmist said, "Yea, though I

58

walk through the valley of the shadow of death, I will fear no evil: for Thou art with me . . ." (23:4). Moffatt translates that to read "glen of gloom." It means those difficult, heartbreaking experiences of life, from which we shrink. They may be death, or sickness, or the loss of a job, or many things. But notice that word "through." If we are sure that we will go through, we can stand anything. And the assurance of God's companionship is our assurance of "getting through."

Sometimes we wonder why certain things happen. But as Whittier expressed it:

> Yet in the maddening maze of things
> And tossed by storm and flood,
> To one fixed ground my spirit clings;
> I know that God is good . . .
> —*The Eternal Goodness*

And knowing that, we know that within His will things do eventually work out right. Thus we are not afraid of tomorrow.

You Gain A Victory

Regardless of the circumstances of one's life or the difficulties one is called upon to face, I firmly believe God can and will bring any person through to victory, if—and that "if" should be underscored—*if* the person is surrendered to God's will.

A man named Harry wrote his life's story and entitled it *My Wheelchair to the Stars*. You don't usually think of climbing to the stars in a wheelchair, but Harry did. At seven years of age, he had rheumatic fever and later he developed severe arthritis. His pain was such that often even the wearing of clothes was a torture.

His father and mother worked in a textile mill and had no choice but to leave him at home sitting in his wheelchair. As Harry grew older, his illness got into his mind. He began to worry that his life counted for so little. He began to feel there was no reason for living, that he could never be anything except a burden on his parents. He became fearful of what would become of him when they died.

One day he had a particularly bitter experience. He fell out of his chair and lay on the floor helpless for several hours. He said, "I couldn't rise. I struggled and sweated and wept. There on the floor I battled again and again the black wave of bitterness. If I ever prayed, I prayed then. Eventually the postman came. I yelled for him and he came in and picked me up. That postman said, Harry, "with God all things are possible" [Mark 10:27].

These words burned themselves into Harry's mind. They drove out the black waves of bitterness. Someone suggested that he paint Christmas cards. He worked six months to make his first card, which would sell for a nickel. But he kept at it, and one year he made $800 from his greeting cards. Then he dared take a reckless plunge. He persuaded his father and mother to mortgage their little home for $2,800. With that, he borrowed $1,000 more to finance a mail order greeting card business. His mother asked, "If you don't sell the cards you have bought, what then?" He simply said, "With God all things are possible." He did sell the cards.

He says he will never forget the first year he did a

million dollars worth of business and he said, "I went to the stars in a wheelchair." He ended his story by thanksgiving for his struggles, which God's power had been sufficient to see him through.

Surrender to God's will also gives one a high purpose in life. Our Lord said, ". . . he that loseth his life for my sake shall find it" (Matthew 10:39). Archibald Rutledge told of an old man who ran the engines on a tugboat. The engines were kept spotlessly clean and in the man's face was a radiant glow. In explaining to Mr. Rutledge, he said, "It's this-a-way—I'se got a glory." And having a glory, he had everything.

9.
THE FAITH YOU KEEP
WILL KEEP YOU

THOMAS À KEMPIS expressed one of the fundamental principles of victorious living when he said, "If thou bear the cross, it will soon bear thee." That has been proved again and again. Some time ago, I was in the office of a very successful businessman. It is an elegant office with expensive furnishings, big leather chairs, air-conditioning, and every detail just right. This man has a big business; he is wealthy and highly respected. He has undertaken daring enterprises and has come out on top.

I said, "Tell me the secret of your life." He hesitated

for a few moments; he seemed to be lost in some very sacred memory. Then slowly he began to talk about an older brother who was brilliant and good and was great even at the age of twenty-eight when he died. This man was a boy of only fourteen when his brother got sick. The family was too poor to afford a nurse, and it fell to his lot to nurse his brother.

His brother was sick for months, and there were many unpleasant tasks to perform. In the latter stages of his brother's illness, there were times he could hardly bear to do what needed to be done. But he loved his brother, and he carried out those distasteful tasks without complaint. "Always," he said, "when I had done what I could and the task was finished, I felt good about it. After my brother died, I forgot about the unpleasant part of nursing him and I thought about how glad I was I had done it."

Later on this boy grew to manhood, but life did not come easy for him. There were a lot of hard jobs to be done, a lot of times when he wanted to give up and quit. But day by day, he did his best at the job before him. And then, when he went to bed at night, he felt good inside. He knew he had done what he should have. He learned and practiced one of life's greatest truths: The cross bears those who bear the cross.

Leaving his office, I began thinking of how St. Paul expressed it. He simply said, ". . . I have kept the faith" (II Timothy 4:7). Those words come near the end of probably the last letter the Apostle ever wrote. Soon afterward he was led from his prison cell and executed. He was writing to his young friend, Timothy, telling him to stand firm always, hold true to the course, endure the afflictions.

62

Now as an old man, St. Paul can look back and see many times when he was tempted to give up, but day by day, through each hard experience, he "kept the faith." Now at the end of the way, though his friends have deserted him, he points out, "Demas hath forsaken me" —"Alexander the coppersmith did me much evil"—"No man stood with me." But in spite of everything, he is serene and not afraid.

He says, "Notwithstanding the Lord stood with me. . . ." (4:17). At the end of the way, when the going is the roughest, we see that the faith he kept, kept him.

A very wise man who had spent his life dealing with people once said to me, "Every person who attained greatness had to fight the temptation of committing suicide." Maybe for most of us the temptation has not been that extreme, but certainly time after time we are tempted to give up and quit. In fact, most of us have at times given up. Not many can look back over all the experiences of life and say with St. Paul, "I have kept the faith."

There have been times when we have not been our best. Of those times we are ashamed. But, thank God, we can also look back upon times when we did "keep the faith." Of those times we are very proud. The victories we have won are now our strongest supports. The faith we kept is keeping us—the crosses we bore are now bearing us.

Max Beerbohm wrote a story called "The Happy Hypocrite." It is about Lord George Hell, who was an unscrupulous villain. Not only was he mean inside, he looked the part outside. Just seeing his face made people afraid of him. He fell in love with a young girl, Little Miss Mere, who was both beautiful and innocent.

She refused him, however, because as she said, "I can never be the wife of a man whose face is not saintly."

Because he wanted her so much, Lord George Hell had the finest maskmaker make him a mask that was saintly. With the mask of a saint, he again sought the love of Miss Mere and won it, and they were married. Day by day he sought to keep up his hypocrisy. He was careful to be unselfish, attentive, and patient. He constantly held in check his evil tendencies in order to appear a saint.

But one day an old enemy found him, and in the presence of his lovely wife, ruthlessly tore off Lord Hell's mask. But when the mask was removed, a saint's face was revealed. He had actually become what he had practiced being day by day. The faith that he had kept, at the last kept him.

Practice keeping faith day by day, and one day you will have enough to keep you.

Look Back and Remember

There are three thoughts to keep in mind, which will help us to keep our faith. The first is: when tempted to give up or lose faith, look back and remember the times you won the victory. Maybe it was some crisis fifteen years ago. You did not see how you could go on, but you did go on and it worked out all right. You discovered new courage and strength inside you that you did not know you had.

Later some other crisis came into your life. You did not see a chance for yourself, but you kept holding on. Maybe some friend helped you that you had not counted on. Anyway, you got through it. Some time later, still another crisis developed. You can't explain it, but as you kept walking through the dark, suddenly you came out into the sunshine. It seemed to work out providentially. As you look back now, you decide it *was* providential.

We do have unused inner resources; there are friends who help; God does take a hand in our lives. And somehow we eventually come to believe that no matter what life does to us, we can go on. That belief helps us to keep the faith.

Forces That Uphold Us

St. Paul said, ". . . I have kept the faith," and in the end, the faith that he kept, kept him. But sometimes it seems almost impossible to keep faith. Remembering the past victories we have won will help us to keep from giving up in some new crisis. A second help in keeping the faith is not to forget that, though life has a way of pulling us down, there are even stronger forces in life that hold us up. Life may hurt us, but even more it aids us.

Some years ago, one of the great Sequoia trees in California was cut down. Scientists studied the tree and then told us something of its history. It was a seedling 271 years before Christ was born; 516 years later, it was severely damaged in a forest fire, but nature immediately set to work to repair the damage. Though it was hurt, the tree kept living and growing, and a hundred years later the scar caused by the fire was completely covered. In later years, two other fires damaged the tree, but nature worked to heal those, also.

Life has the power to hurt, to hurt deeply; but life also has the power to heal, to heal completely. When you are tempted to give up your faith, remember that life's helping power is stronger than its hurting power.

FAITH HAS WON FOR OTHERS

A third fact to remember when you are tempted not to keep faith is to remember some of the great triumphs faith has won for others, and also remember you are made of the same stuff of which they were made.

Fix in your mind, for example, Mozart. When he was twenty-five, he went to Vienna. There, ten years later, he died. During those ten years he wrote his matchless music, which will live forever. One day his publisher said to him harshly, "Write, sir, in a more easy and popular style; or I will neither print your music nor pay you a penny for it."

Mozart and his wife were so poor that they often had neither food nor fuel in their tiny house. One cold morning that winter, a friend who came to visit Mozart found his house entirely without heat and the composer and his wife waltzing to keep warm. In fact, the cold and hunger put him in his grave when he was thirty-five.

It must have been an almost unbearable temptation to him to sacrifice his standards. He might so easily have said, "After all, a man has to eat." Or even more easily said, "I cannot see my wife suffer." Instead, he said to his publisher, "Then, my good sir, I have only to resign and die of starvation. I cannot write as you demand." And starve he did; but isn't the world proud of him? The faith he kept is still keeping him.

And when you are tempted not to keep your faith, it will help you to remember that within you is something of what was in Mozart. There is something within every person which, if given a chance, will make that person invincible. That something is God, for God is in us.

10.

FAITH IS THE POWER TO HEAL

As you read the Gospels, you never find an instance when Jesus healed without finding the element of faith somewhere in the story. When the paralytic was brought by his friends and let down through the roof into the presence of Jesus, it was faith. Read it—Mark says, "When Jesus saw their faith . . ." (2:5).

Blind Bartimaeus was sitting by the roadside. He cried out to Christ, and his call was returned. Jesus asked, "What wilt thou that I should do unto thee?" He replied, "Lord, that I might receive my sight." There he is expressing belief not only in the power of Christ to heal but also in Christ's willingness to heal him. He was healed. In explanation, Jesus said, ". . . thy faith hath made thee whole" (Mark 10:46-52).

There was the centurion whose servant was sick. Hearing that Jesus was in the vicinity, he sent word asking that the Lord speak the word that would heal his servant. He believed that Christ did not need even to come to his house. The servant was healed. Jesus said,

"... I have not found so great faith. .." (Luke 7:1-10).

There was the cripple at the pool of Bethesda. For thirty-eight years he had been there. He made all manner of excuses about himself. Jesus merely asked one question: "Wilt thou be made whole?" That is, do you really want to be well? Is your mind concerned with the picture of health? His healing was dependent on his own faith (John 5:1-8).

One of the tenderest expressions of faith is seen in the story of the woman who touched the hem of His garment. For twelve years she had been sick. But she wanted so much to be well. Instead of resigning herself to her sickness, all those years she had done all she could to get well. Though she had spent everything she had and nothing had helped her, she would not give up.

She had heard stories of the Man of Galilee who could heal. Not only did she hear, she also believed. She said, "If I may touch but his clothes, I shall be whole." She did touch the hem of His garment, and she was made well. What did Jesus say to her? "Daughter, thy faith hath made thee whole ..." (Mark 5:25-34).

Immediately following that story is the record of a father who came to Jesus about his daughter. To him Jesus said, "Be not afraid, only believe" (Mark 5:36).

In our conflict between science and superstition, which has been wrongly interpreted as a conflict between science and religion, we came to a day when science raised its flag of victory. But now we are not sure. Perhaps there is no power in wearing a string of amber-colored beads to ward off certain diseases; yet science is coming to realize there was tremendous power in the faith of the person wearing those beads.

How Does Faith Heal?

There are many answers. For one, let us begin with a definition of faith: "Now faith is the substance of things hoped for, the evidence of things not seen" (Hebrews 11:1). In reference to healing, that means that though you are sick, you hope to be well; in spite of your illness, you believe in health. Faith pictures recovery in the sick person's mind. And that is powerful.

The architect gains strength for long, tedious drawing because he pictures in his mind the completed cathedral. Columbus had strength to overcome opposition, to keep on sailing west, in spite of conditions that would have caused almost any person to give up and quit, because in his mind he pictured land ahead.

Before any sick person can ever be well, he must picture health in his mind and believe it can be achieved. That is faith. There is a story of the barber in a small town courting the librarian. For years the folks of the community watched as each afternoon he came by the library to walk home with her. On summer evenings they could be seen sitting together on her porch; in the winter in the parlor.

The town was concerned and felt it would be a good marriage, but the barber could never get quite enough courage to ask the all-important question. Then one day, a dashing, romantic salesman moved into the community. He went one day to borrow a book, and as often happens, he became more interested in the librarian than in the library.

More and more he dropped around to borrow books, and one afternoon the librarian told the barber she would be busy that night. She began being busy a lot of nights. The barber became worried. The entire town began to talk. The barber decided to talk the matter over with his friend, the druggist.

He explained to the druggist how much he loved the girl, that he wanted to marry her, but that his courage failed when it came time to ask her. The druggist explained that he could fix him a capsule that would be just what the barber needed. The capsule was made and the druggist told him that it would act powerfully about fifteen minutes after he took it.

That night he was to see the librarian. He took the capsule as he started to her house and by the time he got there his courage had so developed that he rushed in, grabbed the librarian by the arm and firmly announced, "Come on, we're going to get married." And they did.

A few days later, he said to the druggist, "That was the most powerful capsule I ever took. What was in it?" The druggist smiled and quietly replied, "Three things —first, a gelatin capsule; second, some sugar; third, the belief that you could do it."

The third ingredient was the one that mattered. Belief or faith is usually the ingredient that makes the difference between success and failure—between being well and being sick.

A college friend of mine, Dr. Carl J. Sanders, now a distinguished pastor in Virginia, tells of one of his members who was carried into the operating room in a Richmond hospital for surgery. As they were preparing to give him the anesthesia, the patient turned to the doctor and nervously asked, "Doctor, do you think I will die on the operating table?"

"Indeed I do not. Why?" demanded the doctor.

"I just can't get over the feeling that I am going to die during the operation," the patient insisted.

The doctor ordered the patient taken back to his room. He had his pastor, Dr. Sanders, called and that afternoon the patient and the pastor were alone together. They talked about God and about faith. The next morning the patient was again carried to the operating room, but now he carried faith with him and the surgeon had no hesitation in going on with the operation.

The point being: science at its best is now realizing that without faith it is insufficient.

Admiral Du Pont was explaining to Admiral Farragut the reasons why he had failed to enter Charleston Harbor with his fleet of ironclads. Farragut listened until he was through, and then said, "Du Pont, there is one reason more."

"What is that?" questioned Du Pont.

"You did not believe you could."

On one occasion it was even said of Jesus that He could do no mighty works because of the unbelief of the people. It was in His own home town. "Is not this the carpenter's son?" (Matthew 13:55) they said with contempt. They knew His brothers and sisters. They recognized Him only as an ordinary person among them. And because they had no faith in Him, they failed to experience His miracle-working power (Matthew 13:54-58).

If you do not believe in the power of Christ to heal, it is certain that you will never experience His power. The Bible tells us that: "But without faith it is impossible to please him: for he that cometh to God must believe that he is, and that he is a rewarder of them that diligently seek him" (Hebrews 11:6).

Mussolini made a sorry mess of his life but at least he

71

expressed one great truth. He said: "The capacity of modern man to believe is unbelievable."

The extent to which you can believe if you will only let yourself will amaze you. Perhaps your faith is small, but Christ is *not* small. And remember: It is not a perfect faith that heals—it is a perfect Saviour who heals. But He needs what faith you have.

FAITH CREATES A PICTURE OF HEALTH

Faith creates a mental picture of health, and without a healthy attitude of mind, nobody can be healthy. As Leslie Weatherhead put it: "Sometimes it is more important to know what kind of a fellah has a germ, than what kind of a germ has a fellah."

There are germs and sickening circumstances in every life. But inner faith is stronger than outward circumstances. As Dr. Harry Emerson Fosdick said it: "Fear imprisons, faith liberates; fear paralyzes, faith empowers; fear disheartens, faith encourages; and most of all, fear puts hopelessness into the heart of life, while faith rejoices in its God."

Faith begins where physical resources leave off. Annie Johnson Flint says it well:

When we have exhausted our store of endurance,
When our strength has failed ere the day is half done,
When we reach the end of our hoarded resources,
Our Father's full giving is only begun.
                                      —*He Giveth More*

Louis Binstock tells a marvelous story of the power of

faith. A little girl living on the Gaspé Peninsula in Quebec had contracted a rare disease which only rest, time, and the will to live could cure. But the child was so enamored of the statue of Saint Anne she could see from her window that she made no effort to recover. Death, she felt, would unite her with her saintly friend.

Desiring to die, she became weaker every day. To the priest she said, "If the Saint does not wish me to die, she will give me some sign."

A few nights later the little girl was awakened by the sound of glorious organ music. She looked through the window and saw the statue of Saint Anne radiantly transfused in silvery light. "That is the sign!" she exclaimed. "The Saint wants me to live." Immediately she began to get well. The people of the town became excited over the wonderful miracle.

The priest called the people together and told them how it had actually happened. The sign had been arranged. Knowing how the full moon always bathed the statue of Saint Anne, he had slipped into the church to play the organ at the right moment and had awakened the child.

The people were resentful. They did not want to give up their miracle. To them the priest said, "I know how you feel. But some day you will understand you have beheld a far greater miracle." Instead of the organ music and the lighted statue, something that could be explained merely by a full moon and an organist playing, they had seen the miracle of the power of faith within that sick little girl.

Jesus still walks through the crowds. But only those with a deep hunger for healing, those who with deep sincerity reach out by faith to Him, ever hear Him saying, ". . . thy faith hath made thee whole; go in peace . . ." (Mark 5:34).

II.

MIRACLE DRUGS FOR THE SOUL

RECENTLY a close friend of mine was granted $65,000 for research to seek to discover new medicines for mental illnesses. I shall enjoy discussing with him his work and watching his progress. During the past several years, I have been fascinated by the remarkable progress being made in the treatment of mental diseases.

A short generation ago, when the word "health" was mentioned, we thought only of physical health. As far as the mind was concerned, there were only two kinds of people—the sane and the insane. The treatment for the insane was to put them away where they would not be dangerous. Now we are realizing that there are degrees of mental illness and that often such an illness can be successfully treated and cured.

In recent years much has been learned about emotional illness. We now know that a person may be healthy physically and mentally and yet be ill emotionally. Some emotional illnesses are of such an extent that one cannot live normally or happily. Medical science is giving increased attention to mental and emotional diseases. Much research is being done in these fields; there are an increasingly large number of physicians who are exclusively treating people who are healthy physically but sick in other ways.

We are also realizing that there is another area of sickness. One might be physically, mentally, and emotionally normal but be spiritually sick. Not only are ministers giving much attention to the area of spiritual health, but also this subject is discussed among many physicians and those who are doing scientific research. In fact, many of us believe that spiritual health is the basis of all health.

Some time ago, I wrote a book on the miracles of Christ, the title of which is *The Touch of the Master's Hand*. As I restudied the Lord's miracles, I was amazed at how many of them resulted from spiritual healing. For example, there was the paralyzed man who was let down through the roof (Mark 2:1-12). This man could not walk; he was a physical invalid. But Christ saw beyond his physical illness and saw it was caused by his spiritual illness. So Jesus said, "Son, thy sins be forgiven thee." Through spiritual healing, the man also received physical healing.

Recently I was in another city to preach for five nights. While there I had dinner in the homes of three physicians. These men talked of their work and each mentioned the great value of many new miracle drugs. Diseases that once meant almost certain death can now be healed surely and quickly. As these physicians spoke of how much easier and more effective their work now is with the wonderful new medicines, I found myself wishing I had some miracle drugs for the soul. I thought of such very different things as hatred and sorrow, pride and fear, guilt and indifference. Then I realized we do have drugs that can cure the soul.

Today we are delighted to have miracle drugs for physical, mental and emotional illnesses. But the worst sickness is spiritual sickness. We have cures for that, too. Let me list some cures for soul-sickness.

(1) One is *humility*. Study Jesus' dealings with spiritually sick people and you will see that never could He do anything with a proud man. On one occasion a young man came to Jesus asking, ". . . what good thing shall I do, that I may have eternal life?" (Matthew 19:16). I don't think he was asking how he might get to heaven. Rather, I think he was seeking to possess real life as he had seen it in Jesus. I have heard people say, "I'm not really living." That is how that man felt.

This man said that he had lived a good, moral life but he had missed something that he wanted. Jesus knew of this man's possessions and the pride he had in them. So he told him to give what he had away and then follow Him. Jesus never objected to a man's wealth, except when that wealth gave him a false sense of security and importance.

St. Augustine, in *The City of God,* said that the world has been controlled by two parties: Those who have governed by "love of self to the point of contempt of God" and those who have governed by "love of God to the point of contempt of self."

It has been well said that humility is not thinking poorly of yourself. Humility is not thinking of yourself at all.

Sometimes God has a way of putting us on our knees. I have seen some hard experiences come into the lives of people, but I am convinced that anything that makes us humble is a blessing. We have so much today—lots of money, fine cars and houses and clothes, plenty to eat— it is mighty hard to be humble. But when one is sick in spirit, if he can lose himself in dedication, his sickness will be healed.

(2) Another miracle drug for the sick soul is *truth*. I mean the acceptance of the truth about ourselves. That is not easy. When Ralph Barton, one of the most popular of American cartoonists, took his own life, he left this message: "I have run from wife to wife, from house to house, and from country to country in a ridiculous effort to escape from myself. In doing so I am very much afraid I have caused a great deal of unhappiness to those who have loved me . . . No one is responsible for this . . . except myself . . . I've done it because I am fed up with inventing devices for getting through twenty-four hours every day."

When a person has been caught in the clutches of liquor, the hardest step for him to take on the road to recovery is to admit to himself that he needs help. That is true of any sin or sickness. The Bible promises that God will forgive our sins, but first we must confess them —face up to the horrible fact that we have sinned.

I have spent much time counseling with soul-sick people. It is a hard job to get them to take off their masks of pretense. Facing the truth about yourself will work miracles of healing.

(3) *Forgiveness* is a cure for the soul. Forgiveness has two handles—one that we must take hold of for ourselves and one that we must offer to certain other people. Read the four Gospels, and you are impressed with how often Jesus said to a soul-sick person words such as, "Thy

sins be forgiven thee," "Neither do I condemn thee, go and sin no more." Jesus died on a cross that we might have forgiveness. But in order to receive healing power, we must have faith that God will forgive, must repent of our sin, must have faith that God has forgiven. There are many people who are receiving treatment for physical, mental, or emotional illness who are not being cured. Their trouble is deeper. On their heart is the burden of some guilt. There is only one cure and that is the forgiveness of God.

Also, we must forgive. Ill feelings toward any other person will make the one who holds those feelings ill.

(4) Another miracle drug for the soul is *service*. When a person becomes wrapped up in himself, he gets sick in his soul. Everyone has heard the prayer of the old man who prayed: "Lord, bless me and my wife, My son John and his wife, Us four and no more." Farther down the street there lived a couple without children who prayed: "Lord, bless us two, And that will do." Around the corner there lived an old bachelor whose prayer was, "Lord, bless only me, That's as far as I can see."

We remember that our Lord said, "He that findeth his life shall lose it: and he that loseth his life for my sake shall find it" (Matthew 10:39). You never become spiritually whole until you find something to give yourself for.

(5) For the soul that is sick, the finest healing agent is *the Presence of God*. I have seen people try all sorts of things to find spiritual healing and fail. I have even seen the things I have mentioned fail—forgetting self, honestly facing the truth about ourselves, forgiveness both received and given, and unselfish service. They are wonderful healing agents, but no medicine heals in every case. Penicillin does not heal every time.

But there is one cure that never fails. When one honestly seeks the Presence of God and finds Him, he is healed. The Psalmist said:

Bless the LORD, O my soul, and forget not all his benefits: Who forgiveth all thine iniquities; who healeth all thy diseases.

(Psalm 103:2, 3)

12.

PENICILLIN FOR DESPAIR

ABBÉ PIERRE has a phrase—"penicillin for despair." He declares that to be the world's greatest need. I am inclined to agree. Every person who has been plagued by anxious fears feels the need of "penicillin for despair." Certainly Christ felt that need.

As He knelt that night in Gethsemane, the Bible says, he ". . . began to be sore amazed and very heavy" (Mark 14:33). The Revised Version translates that to read, He ". . . began to be greatly amazed and sore troubled." Moffatt's translation gives, ". . . he began to feel appalled and agitated."

Vincent Taylor, the world-famous Greek scholar, says, "Those verbs denote distress which follows a great shock." He points out that hundreds and thousands of British people are still suffering from the shock of the last war, though many of them do not realize it. Likewise, there are many in America who are still suffering from the shock of that war. And there are numerous other shocks that have come into the personal lives of people.

I have had many people talk to me about how they went to bed only to toss and turn for hours before sleep would come; others of how they suddenly began to tremble, or break into a cold sweat, or feel constant fatigue, or have an abnormal dryness in the mouth, or a palpitating heart, or a constant headache, or a deadness of feeling when they seemed to lose ability to love their own family, even God. Some have even told me about inclinations to suicide.

For people who know the sufferings brought by anxious fears, I have deep sympathy. I have had some of those same feelings. Nearly every normal person has at some time been very heavy—greatly distressed—troubled—appalled—agitated. Some people seem condemned to live with an anxiety neurosis as a constant companion.

In times of anxious strain we are told to "have faith" and all our troubles will magically disappear. That is simply not true. Jesus had faith, but He also knew the meaning of naked terror. Some of the greatest saints have cried out for a "penicillin for despair," yet they also had faith.

We are told that our fears are imaginary. That is a misstatement. All fears are real—none are imaginary. It may be that imagination caused our fears, or it may be that we reacted in the wrong way to some circumstance of life, but the fears themselves are not imaginary.

We are told to "pull ourselves together," but we are not sure what that means. Many do not feel they have strength enough to pull even if they knew what to pull on.

When we have infections of certain types, the physician gives us penicillin and soon the infection is gone.

When you feel despair, or deep anxiety, or trembling fear, or nervous strain, what attitude should you take toward it? Examine the experience of Christ when He felt "very heavy." You will find it in Mark 14:32-36.

We know that Christ was God and that as God He had supernatural insight and power. But also Christ was man, and as man He experienced our same hungers and thirsts. He endured temptation that was real. He had human desires. Also, He had experiences of deep anxiety and despair.

Thus we know that anxious fears may come even though one does have faith. We should not feel ashamed because of nervous symptoms. These experiences come to nearly everyone. But there is such a thing as "penicillin for despair." It isn't a pill or a shot in the arm; it is an action or a series of actions. In His moment of despair, Christ did these three things:

HE GOT ALONE

That night in Gethsemane He moved a distance from the crowd and took with Him His three closest friends. There are times when it is good for us to be with crowds. There are other times when we need to be with some trusted and close friends. Jesus, no doubt, talked with these three about His troubles. Often that helps. It is wonderful to have a friend to share our deepest thoughts. Often it helps to talk with a minister or a competent counselor. But then Jesus went further alone. It is important to see this.

When one is in some dark valley, his first impulse is to tell his troubles to every person who will listen. The reason we want to tell our troubles is because we want sympathy; we get soothing satisfaction from the pity of others and from self-pity. We deny this, but it is true.

The more we talk about our troubles, the worse they become. Speech has a much greater effect on the emotions than thinking has. We can talk ourselves into almost anything, and the more we talk our troubles, the worse they become. Jesus got alone.

He Looked to God

"And he said, Abba, Father, all things are possible unto thee . . ." (Mark 14:36). He took His mind off Himself, and that does much to relieve one of anxiety and fear. But it is hard to do because part of the mind wants to hold onto its worries and despair. That is the easiest way out. To despair is to lose hope, and to lose hope is to be able to give up and quit.

Frequently we translate our despair into bodily illness. Maybe we don't become invalids, but we never "feel well." Much of the sickness of people is merely an escape from reality, the easiest way out. But this is never a final solution. Deep down we are ashamed of our cowardice. We feel guilty for selling our courage to buy sympathy.

When one looks into the face of God, he has hope because he does know that "all things are possible unto" Him.

When Jesus "began to be sore amazed and very

heavy"—distressed, troubled, and despairing, He did three things: He got alone; He looked into the face of God; and

HE TOOK POSITIVE ACTION

In the midst of despair, the great temptation is to retire, to slip into illness, to surrender. It is a great struggle to do something. It was a struggle for our Lord. Luke vividly portrays the strain Christ was under. He says, ". . . his sweat was as it were great drops of blood falling down to the ground" (Luke 22:44). But in spite of the struggle, Jesus centered His mind on something to do. He refused to retire into Himself.

Activity is often the best cure for the blues. Physicians tell us that our fear thoughts come from the higher brain centers while physical activity comes from the lower brain centers. When one begins to exercise those lower brain centers through activity, it lessens the tension of the upper brain centers. I have read of operations by which certain parts of the brain are removed to lessen those fear thoughts. I knew of a man who took daily exercise. He said it "straightened out his thoughts."

What did Jesus do? He prayed, "not my will, but thine, be done." He committed Himself wholly to the will of God. There is the faith that is the answer to fear. It lifts one's thoughts away from his own troubles and centers his mind on the strength of God.

It has been truly said, "In His will is our peace." That is the "penicillin for despair." Commitment to His will cures despair and brings peace for several reasons: it takes from us the fear of getting lost; it relieves us of the burden of the responsibility of tomorrow; it gives us the approval of a good conscience; it gives us a constructive life to live. Dedication to His will enables us to say with the Psalmist, "Yea, though I walk through the valley of the shadow of death, I will fear no evil: for thou art with me . . ." (23:4). Realizing that He is with us, we have confidence that we will get through even the worst experience. Thus there is no room in our minds for despair.

13.
DON'T LET YOUR DEFEATS DEFEAT YOU

IN MANY WAYS the minister must learn to say to people, "Don't let your defeats defeat you." I read the many letters that come, but none of them ever say, "This has been such a happy day in my life, I wanted to write you about it."

No one ever phones to say, "My marriage is so perfect I called to tell you about it." Nobody ever comes by to say, "God has so abundantly blessed me that I have more money than I can spend." No—the minister hears about the heartaches, the broken dreams, the poverty, the disappointments.

It seems that everybody is in some way defeated in life and, as a matter of fact, everybody is. Some have much harder defeats than do others—but along the way every person meets a defeat. In his book, *The Christ of the Round Table,* E. Stanley Jones tells about a man standing to say during a discussion, "For me Christianity means victory—victory—victory." But quickly another rose and stated, "For me it means victory—defeat—victory." Then a third added, "For me it means defeat—victory—defeat."

Surely most of us would confess that life is not a series of unbroken victories. Generously mixed in with our triumphs are many defeats. Sometimes we fail when we have done our very best; sometimes we fail because we didn't do our best.

Several months ago, I was preaching in another city. In the audience was a minister whom I consider one of the greatest in America. He has a great mind and a deep consecration. After the meeting he came up and suggested we slip out together for a cup of coffee and a visit. I was delighted and honored to be in his presence. He is the kind of a minister I would like to be.

In a quiet corner of the little restaurant, we talked of many things, but eventually began to confess our faults to each other. That is a dangerous thing to do. You know the story of the three ministers who were traveling together and decided to confess their faults to each other. One named his faults, the second named his, and they were both pretty bad. They turned to the third who until then had been silent. He said, "My worst fault is gossiping, and I can't wait until I get back home."

But this minister told me of the struggles he has had to control his emotions of fear and anger. Sometimes he feels an overwhelming fear just before he is to speak. It is a burden to him. Sometimes he has great difficulty controlling his anger. He told me that we needed to invent an "ecclesiastical profanity," so that he could express himself at times. Of course, he was partly joking.

Then very seriously he said, "Only Christ perfectly mastered life. Even the best Christians among us have pagan intervals." By that he meant, no one is perfectly good. We all have defeats, but defeats can be blessings.

One of my favorite books in the Bible is Hebrews. It was written to a small band of people who were discouraged. They had been converted from one religious group to Christianity. When they left their own group, their old friends and even their own families had turned against them! They found it hard to make a living and they faced bitter persecution.

The Book of Hebrews contains the most eloquent statement on faith ever recorded anywhere. It is the eleventh chapter, which begins, "Now faith is the substance of things hoped for, the evidence of things not seen." That chapter goes on to tell of the struggles of great people in history and how, by faith, they won mighty victories. To these people the writer is saying, hold onto your faith and you will not be finally defeated.

The next chapter begins by telling them how they can hold their faith—by remembering those who gained victories, by turning away from that besetting sin, by being patient day by day, but mainly by, "Looking unto Jesus the author and finisher of our faith. . . ." Now notice the next words about Jesus. "Who was the greatest teacher of all time"—no, that is not what it says. "Who had the power to perform mighty miracles"—no, that is not mentioned. This is what it says: ". . . who for the joy that was set before him endured the cross. . . ." He knew the meaning of deep suffering and sorrow.

Then we read in the twelfth chapter these words: "My son, despise not thou the chastening of the Lord. . . . For whom the Lord loveth he chasteneth. . . ." Sometimes God puts us on our backs in order to make us look up. Sometimes it is just the circumstances of life that bring our disappointing defeats. But remember, don't let your defeats defeat you.

BE RECEPTIVE

Defeats can bless you because they make you more receptive to God.

The Book of Hebrews tells us, "By faith Moses . . . endured, as seeing him who is invisible" (11:23, 27). Where did Moses get that faith? It came out of his defeat. Once he lost his temper and did wrong. As a result, he became a fugitive. At the age of forty, he was a penniless, broken failure. He had lived in a palace, but now he had to take a job as a sheepherder.

Out on the range one day, he saw a bush on fire. It was strange because the bush never burned up. He went to investigate and there he heard the voice of God. He listened to God and obeyed, and he went on to great victories. Had it not been for the chastening of a defeat, he would never have heard and responded to God.

After World War II, we sent teachers to Japan to help rebuild the country. One of those teachers remarked, "It is so much easier to teach a defeated country because it knows its methods must have been wrong. A victorious country is prone to feel it has been right and does not care to learn new things."

87

Sometimes we have to be defeated before we listen to God.

A famous golf champion said that he learned from his defeats, never from his victories. After he had been defeated in a tournament, he would go to some golf teacher and say, "Tell me what I am doing wrong." Then he would work to correct his mistakes.

Likewise when defeats come in life, we are more prone to come to God for correction and instruction. Maurice Maeterlinck said, "Beauty and grandeur are all about us but only when some emergency or disaster cracks the shell of life do we grope our way upward to catch the gleams which come through the cracks."

BE RESOURCEFUL

If we refuse to be defeated by our defeats, they will make us more resourceful. Booker T. Washington spoke of the "advantage of a disadvantage." He himself was an example. He was born a slave, and one of his jobs was to carry the books of the white children to school. He had no books of his own, and he was not permitted inside the school. But he developed a passion for education and he later became one of the best-educated men of his day. He devoted his life to making an education possible for those of his race.

Often when we have failed in some way, we realize our own strengths are not sufficient. Then we discover the resources and strengths of the spiritual. We recall the name of Joseph Goebbels, who was Hitler's chief assistant. In his diary he made several references to Gandhi and each time refers to him as a fool and a fanatic. But through physical force, Goebbels failed; through spiritual power, Gandhi won his life's victory.

Sometimes we must fail before we are willing to discover our spiritual resources.

Become Redemptive

Not only do our defeats make us more receptive and more resourceful; what is more important, they make us more redemptive.

Who is the most beloved American of all time? His mother died when he was a baby. He had very little opportunity to go to school and to prepare himself. He ran for the legislature but was defeated. He entered business but a worthless partner put him into bankruptcy. He loved a girl dearly, but she died. Later he married another, but it was an unhappy marriage.

He served one term in Congress but was defeated for reelection. He worked for an appointment to the United States Land Office but did not get it. He tried to be a lyceum lecturer but failed. He ran for the Senate but was defeated. He ran for the office of Vice-President but was defeated. His name is Abraham Lincoln. He "endured chastening," and who can deny that he became a true son of God?

I read of a shepherd who broke the leg of a wayward lamb. Through nursing it back to health, the shepherd knew he would win the lamb to obedience to his voice. And through our defeats, God often nurses us to obedience to Him.

14.

POWER TO DESTROY THE EVIL WITH WHICH YOU LIVE

FUTURE HISTORIANS will probably describe the time in which we are now living as the age of power. We have seen the beginning of the use of atomic power, the development of electric power, and mechanical engines with tremendous power. And now we are learning to utilize power drawn from the rays of the sun. Today man has at his disposal unmeasured power.

Our generation is also making great progress in the field of spiritual and personal power. Some of the best thinkers in the world today are studying the individual man, his weaknesses and needs, his sources of inner strength and power. And we are beginning to develop a clearer understanding of Christ and what He taught than the world has ever had before.

For example, today we are looking at Luke 10:19 with new light and understanding. Jesus said: "Behold, I give unto you power to tread on serpents and scorpions, and over all the power of the enemy; and nothing shall by any means hurt you." That verse has been misunderstood by certain ignorant and fanatical people, and they have developed a religious sect called "snake-handlers." This practice is so repulsive to normal people that we have looked away from that verse and wished it were not in the Bible. Actually it is one of the most wonderful promises our Lord gave to us.

When Jesus said "serpents and scorpions," He was speaking in parables, referring to those sinister, slimy things that slither through your life—the things that strike you down and poison your very soul. Please pardon me for even mentioning the idea, but if you were forced to live in a house in which you knew there was a snake, you would never have an easy moment. That very thought causes us to cringe. Yet, that is a picture of many lives. They are forced to live with some sinister weakness that sets up constant dread in their minds.

I have come to know many people who must live with some serpent. There is the one with a suicidal tendency always lurking in the shadows. In moments of stress and strain it strikes, sometimes with fatal consequences. One of the most pitiful people in our society is the sex pervert. We normally have contempt for homosexuals, yet for some of those people it is an awful burden to bear. There is the alcoholic who goes along for weeks and sometimes even years, and then suddenly in an unguarded moment the thing strikes.

People live with other serpents, such as deep feelings of inadequacy and inferiority. Others live with abnormal fears that cause them to break out in cold sweats. Some are extremely sensitive to criticism. The other day I saw a group of children afflicted with cerebral palsy. They lack muscular control. I know people who seem to lack emotional control. In many lives there is hate and prejudice.

But Jesus promised power over all these "serpents and scorpions." Instead of being hurt by them, we can overcome and destroy them.

The Armor of the Spirit

Jesus promises us power over the weaknesses and sinister enemies of our lives and says, ". . . nothing shall by any means hurt you."

That does not mean that all your weaknesses will suddenly be taken away. It does not mean that you will not get some injury from life, that you will not experience disappointment, that you will not get sick or grow old. But it does mean that you can have the kind of power that is stronger than those things. You can be clad in an armor, not of steel, but an armor of the spirit, and the enemies of life cannot break through to really hurt you. With the power of Christ, you will not be destroyed or dethroned from the mastery of your life.

In connection with this power over life's enemies, Christ also promises power to gain thrilling victories in the conquests of life. Speaking to His disciples, Christ said, "But ye shall receive power, after that the Holy Ghost is come upon you . . ." (Acts 1:8). He was speaking to very ordinary men, men with all the human weaknesses that people have today. But Jesus is saying, "You men will become endowed with extraordinary power so that you can accomplish things you never dreamed of accomplishing before—you can even conquer the world."

The story of how those men did go out and "turn the world upside down" is well known. They became irresistible. So it has continued through the years. For example, in the little city of Assisi, there lived a gay youth by the name of Francis. He lived for pleasure and the satisfaction of his physical appetites. Francis was not satisfied with himself, but he seemed unable to change his ways.

One day he attended a little church. He came as most people come to church, not expecting anything to happen. The priest was reading some passage of the Scripture, when the miracle happened. The cold print of the Bible suddenly began to live for Francis. The life leaped from the printed page into his heart, and he became a transformed person. He began to preach with such winsome beauty and effectiveness that he transformed the life of his day. What happened? He became the possessor of a mighty spiritual power.

A story is told about an old preacher who visited Aldersgate Street Church in London. He knew it was the church where John Wesley had received that marvelous experience through which his heart had become "strangely warmed." He knew how Wesley had gone out from there, the possessor of a power so warm and yet so strong that through his preaching the moral tone of all England was changed and a worldwide revival was begun.

This devout old preacher asked the exact spot in the church where Wesley had been sitting when it happened. Reverently he sat down, lifted up his eyes and fervently prayed, "O Lord, do it again—do it again." And to this very hour, God is doing it again for those who really want to receive His Power.

How You can Get This Power

"Behold, I give you power," Christ said. Again he promised, "ye shall receive power." And His promises hold good for any person today just as they did for those to whom He first spoke those words.

If you want the power of Christ in your life—power to overcome those things that hurt you and power to give you victory in life—how can you get it? All power is channeled to us through mechanisms. Man learned how to build electric generators and thereby made electric power available. The scientists gave us the formula for atomic power, and we build the plants to produce it.

And the mechanism through which man receives the power of God is the experience we call conversion. We remember that one night a man by the name of Nicodemus came to Jesus. He said to Christ, ". . . no man can do these miracles that thou doest, except God be with him" (John 3:2). Nicodemus recognized in Christ the power of God. He was asking how he, too, might have that power.

Jesus said, ". . . ye must be born again" (3:7). That is, you must become a different person. But how can that be accomplished? Nicodemus asked. Jesus did not explain. Instead, he pointed out that the wind blows but we do not know where it comes from or where it goes. Yet we know it blows. Likewise, the Spirit of God comes into our lives, but we cannot explain exactly how that happens.

Then Jesus spoke the most marvelous word this world has ever heard: "For God so loved the world, that he gave his only begotten Son, that whosoever believeth in him should not perish, but have everlasting life" (John 3:16).

There are those who admit, "I do need to change," and they set in to change themslves. They quit this and they quit that. They resolve to do this and to do that. But they find that their self-improvement programs just do not work. But when by faith they believe in Christ and accept Him as their Saviour, the miracle happens. As a result of yielding ourselves to Christ two things happen:

(1) We turn loose of those things in our lives that are wrong. We realize that evil in our lives blocks out the power of God, and we are led to turn from our wicked ways. Remember, when you take hold of Christ, you turn loose of the wrong you have been doing. To surrender to Christ also means to surrender those things that are not according to His Spirit.

(2) When you accept Christ, His will becomes your will and in all things and in every situation you say, "What would Christ do?" As best you understand it, you seek to live as He would live if He were in your place. You pray as He prayed: ". . . nevertheless not my will, but thine, be done" (Luke 22:42). With the surrendering of your evil ways and of your life to the will of God, there begins to flow into your life the power of God.

15.

CHANGE YOUR THOUGHTS
AND YOU CHANGE YOURSELF

MOST PEOPLE would like to change something in their lives. Some people would like to change almost everything in their lives. The Bible teaches us that to change what we want to change, we must change our thoughts. To see this truth, we need to understand three great Bible texts.

The first one: "For as he thinketh in his heart, so is he" (Proverbs 23:7). Down through the centuries wise men have said this same thing. Marcus Aurelius has been called the wisest man of the Roman Empire. He said, "Your life is what your thoughts make of it." One of the wisest men who ever lived in America was Ralph Waldo Emerson, who said, "A man is what he thinks about all day long."

Though this principle has been proved through centuries of experience, still multitudes have not yet seen it. We have the idea that our lives are determined not by what we think but rather by what we have. If we could just make more money and buy all the things we want, we think we would have everything necessary to bring happiness and contentment into our lives. So, we expend our energies to possess things; and even if we are successful, we still end up the same frustrated, unhappy people.

Dr. Norman Vincent Peale tells a wonderful story. A barber's supply association was having a convention. Their publicity agent went into the worst section of the city and found the most unpromising specimen of human nature there—a dirty, unshaven, ragged, drunken, sad man. The barbers went to work on him; he was given a bath, haircut, shave, shampoo, facial massage, manicure —the works.

Then he was dressed in fine clothes from top to bottom, fitted by the best tailor. They put a handkerchief, folded just right, in his coat pocket, put on him neat shoes and a proper hat. They provided a smart-looking topcoat and even put a cane in his hand. They photographed each step of this transformation and had the pictures printed in the newspaper. The people were amazed at the change the barbers wrought. He was transformed from a bum in the gutter to one of the finest-looking gentlemen in the city.

One man was so impressed that he offered the man a good job. He was to come to work the next morning at eight o'clock. But he was late. In fact, he didn't show up all day. So the employer went looking for him and he found him down in the same old street, dead drunk, sleeping on some old newspapers in an alley. His fine clothes were rumpled and soiled. The end of the story is, though you may change a person's outside appearance, the man himself remains the same until he is changed inside.

We sometimes think that our lives are determined by the circumstances that surround us. Actually, the opposite is true. The kind of person you are determines the circumstances about you. If you want a better life, the place to change is inside yourself.

THE RENEWING OF YOUR MIND

The way to change your life is to change your thoughts. St. Paul said it better. He said, ". . . be ye transformed by the renewing of your mind . . ." (Romans 12:2). We make a great mistake when we belittle the power of our thoughts. God gave man a marvelous body, but the most wonderful thing man possesses is his brain.

A scientist once stated: "If you took all the electronic equipment in the United States and put it all together, you would not have as complicated a machine as is one human brain." In California, I had dinner one night with a man who helps build these great computers. He told me that in a matter of seconds, he could work out a problem that would take eighty scientists a lifetime to solve.

On the other hand, a computer lacks the power of thought. It can only work out in a mechanical way the thoughts of some human brain. And no machine can know the thrill of romance, of happy memories, of inspired imagination, and of a deep spiritual experience. But there is this valid comparison—put a human thought into that machine and it will give a certain answer. Put in a different thought and you get a different answer. So it is with life. Your thought determines your answer.

Let me give a simple illustration. One Sunday morning as I was driving to church, I saw the fine building of another church, and many people going in there. On down at the next corner, many, many more people were going into another great church. I noticed a throng of people headed for still another church across the street.

As I drove along, several cars passed me that gave evidence of being in a great hurry. I reasoned they were going to church and they were hurrying to get a seat. I found myself getting a little uneasy. I began to think, everybody is going to these other churches and there will be nobody coming to my church. Then I began to think up some criticisms of those other preachers. I am ashamed to admit it, but human nature works that way, even among preachers.

Then I caught myself. "This is silly for me to think like this, and it isn't my normal way of thinking." Then I started to think of those other ministers and the great work for Christ they are doing. I thought of the loyalty and consecration of the members of those other churches. I began praying that God would especially bless the work of those other men, and I thought of many other ministers of the city.

Then the words of Hebrews 12:1 came to mind: "Wherefore seeing we also are compassed about with so great a cloud of witnesses, let us lay aside every weight. . . ." Instead of becoming jealous, I began to feel more confidence and joy and I was glad that the Lord's work is being carried on by so many people. My entire spirit was changed just because I changed the way I looked at the situation. And not only did I also have a large congregation to preach to, the people said I preached better that day.

The outcome doesn't depend on the situation you face; it depends on how you think about it.

"For as he thinketh in his heart, so is he." What you think is what you are. "Be ye transformed by the renewing of your mind." You change your life by changing your thoughts. The final step in this process is: "Let this mind be in you, which was also in Christ Jesus" (Philippians 2:5).

One of the greatest stories ever written is "The Great Stone Face," by Nathaniel Hawthorne. On the side of the mountain was the face. It was strong, kind, and honorable. Living nearby was a boy by the name of Ernest. Day by day he would look at that face, and he was thrilled by what he saw. Through his boyhood and even after he became a man, Ernest spent many hours gazing upon the face on the mountain.

There was a legend that someday a man would appear in the community who would look exactly like the face. For years that legend had persisted. One day, when the people were discussing the legend, someone suddenly cried out, "Behold, behold, Ernest is himself the likeness of the Great Stone Face." Indeed he was; he had become like his thoughts.

The secret desires of our hearts eventually show up in our very appearance. Once someone wanted Lincoln to meet a certain man. "I do not want to see him," Lincoln said. But his friend protested, "You do not even know him." Lincoln replied, "I do not like his face." "A man cannot be held responsible for his face," the friend said. "Any grown man is responsible for the look on his face," the President insisted. And Lincoln was right. His own face was an example. Although it was homely and rough, in Lincoln's face one sees the very principles of sympathy and honesty that made him the greatest of all Americans.

Some psychologists have made extensive studies, which show that a person's thoughts show up in his features. I have noticed that married couples who have lived together happily and harmoniously over a number of years come to look more like brother and sister than like husband and wife. As they live together, enjoy common experiences, think alike, they tend to look alike.

I have a dear friend. Whenever I am in his presence I feel strangely different. It seems as though Christ is there, too. A man once wrote to Phillips Brooks, "When I hear you preach I somehow forget about you because you make me think of Christ." This friend does that for me. As I have come to know him better, I have learned his secrets.

Through the years, he has read regularly some portion of Matthew, Mark, Luke, or John—the books that tell about Christ. As he reads those stories he pictures himself as present when they happened. He thinks of himself as a personal friend of the Master. Through repeated reading he has become familiar with every detail of Christ's life. He has come to know Christ better than he knows any other man, and he thinks of Christ as being with him at all times.

Whenever he has a decision to make he first asks, "What would Jesus do?" And whatever he believes the answer to that question is, he does just that as best he can. Little by little, the mind of Christ has taken possession of his mind; and as that has happened, his actions and his life have become like Christ.

If you would like to have inner peace and personal power in your life, put before yourself the One who can give it to you. You will be amazed at the change in you when His mind becomes your mind—when you change your thoughts to His thoughts.

16.

THE MAGIC OF BELIEVING

CLAUDE M. BRISTOL asks: "Is there a something, a force, a factor, a power, a science—call it what you will—which a few people understand and use to overcome their difficulties and achieve outstanding success?"

As a newspaper reporter, he studied the religions of the world and watched them operate. In hospitals he saw people die while others who were just as sick got well. He watched football teams win while other teams who had just as good material lost. He studied the lives of the great men and women in all lines of human endeavor. As a result of years of study, he wrote a book on *The Magic of Believing,* in which he says:

> Gradually I discovered that there is a golden thread that runs through all the teachings and makes them work for those who sincerely accept and apply them, and that thread can be named in a single word —belief. It is the same element or factor, belief, which causes people to be cured through mental healing, enables others to climb high the ladder of success . . . there's genuine magic in believing.

Long before Bristol wrote his book, William James, the great psychologist, arrived at the same conclusion. He said, "Our belief at the beginning of a doubtful undertaking is the one thing—notice that carefully—the one thing that assures the successful outcome of our venture."

Long before William James, Jesus Christ said the same thing: "If thou canst believe, all things are possible to him that believeth" (Mark 9:23). It is amazing what belief can accomplish.

One day Andrew brought his brother Simon to Christ. Carefully the Lord sized him up. He saw in him certain weaknesses, but He also saw possibilities. So Christ said to him, "Thou art Simon the son of Jona: thou shalt be called Cephas, which is by interpretation, A stone" (John 1:42). He was saying, "You are one thing now, but I see in you possibilities of being something else. I believe in you." We know that at times the Lord's faith in Peter was severely tried, yet He kept on believing in him and eventually Peter became the man Jesus believed he could be.

Bishop Hazen Werner tells of being in the home of a woman whose husband had just died. She told of her husband's long nights of suffering and how she had cared for him, not having the money to employ a nurse. He wondered how she could have kept going, and she told him that the neighbors had kept their lights burning through the last few nights. She said, "I knew that they were thinking of us, feeling for us. I can't tell you how, but I got strength from it. It kept me up."

The fact that somebody is interested, that somebody cares, that somebody believes in us is often our strongest support.

Every Person Needs to be Believed In

A mother told me about her son, who had completely missed the way. Again and again he had broken her heart. What could she do? I told her that though she could do nothing else, she could keep on believing in him, that the most powerful force in any person's life is the faith that someone has in him. When we lose that, we lose everything.

There is a story told about Rupert Brooke, the great poet. He was about to sail from Liverpool. After he had gotten on board, he became aware that just about everyone there had someone on the dock waving good-bye. He felt a sudden loneliness. Then he spied a little boy—just a street urchin—down on the dock. He went back down the gangplank and found that boy.

"Do you want to earn sixpence?" he asked. "Sure," said the boy. "Well," Brooke is reported to have said, "here it is. When the ship leaves, stand here and wave to me."

As the great ship moved away, the little boy stood there waving a dirty handkerchief. The heart of the poet was warmed and he was helped.

For several years now it has been my privilege to speak to large crowds in many places over the country. Occasionally someone asks me why I don't spend all my time in that way. But above all things else, I want to be pastor of a church. I want to have my own congregation; I want to belong to some people and feel that they belong to me. It means everything to have a congregation of people who claim me as their pastor. They know my faults and weaknesses, yet they pray for me and believe in me. That is worth more than anyone can measure.

One of the saddest lines in the Bible is the word of the Psalmist, "No man cared for my soul" (142:4).

In Robert Sherwood's play, *Abe Lincoln in Illinois*, Abe speaks of Ann Rutledge: "And then—when I saw her, I knew there could be beauty and purity in people, like the purity you sometimes see in the sky at night. When I took hold of her hand, and held it, all fear, all doubt, went out of me. I believed in God. I'd have been glad to work for her until I die, to get for her everything out of life that she wanted. If she thought I could do it, then I could."

We hear a lot said about gossip in the church and criticism of one another, but actually, there isn't much of that. The very basis of the Christian fellowship is that people love and trust each other. And the better we know Christ, the more we believe. Someone has said, "In the company of sinners, He dreamed of saints." To one who had missed the way, He said, "Neither do I condemn thee: go, and sin no more" (John 8:11). He did not minimize her sin, but neither did He minimize her possibilities. Even though He saw her shameful past, He saw her future could be different.

We need somebody to believe in us. We need to learn to believe in other people. But more important, we need to realize the belief Christ has in us and what it means.

BELIEF MAKES DEMANDS

Study carefully the life of Christ, and you will see that never one time did He speak harshly to a sinner. Instead,

He saw in a fallen one new possibilities and He invited that one into the new way. But sometimes it is awfully hard to accept His belief in us, because it is a very demanding thing.

A certain young man came to Him seeking the life that only Christ could give. The story says Jesus loved him, but though He loved with a love that would never let him go, He also loved with a love that would never let him off. He might have said, "Well, I don't expect you to be perfect. I will excuse your sins," but He didn't say that. He said, "If you want to follow me, you must change your life; you must rid yourself of that wrong." The young man turned from Christ and went away (Mark 10:17-22).

We feel His eyes upon us. We realize the possibilities He sees in us. We know He believes we can be something better than what we are. Yet sometimes we don't want to pay the price He demands. We disobey His commands, we fail to live up to His ideals for us, we are ashamed of things we have done yet we are unwilling to change. He reaches out and places a firm hand on our shoulders, but we twist away from that hand. Sometimes we defiantly say, "It's my life; I will live it as I please."

But across nearly two thousand years, Christ has been reaching out to men and expressing His belief in men, and the fact of His belief has been the magic that has changed more lives than anything else this world has ever known. Though Simon Peter failed Him again and again, Christ never let him go. After His resurrection, He still kept believing in Peter. One morning at breakfast He turned to Peter and said, "Simon, son of Jonas, lovest thou me more than these? . . . Feed my lambs" (John

21:15). Not a word of his past failures did Christ speak. Instead, He gave him a purpose, something to live for.

A tornado swept through a town in which a paralyzed mother lay confined to her bed. When the tornado struck she was at home alone with her two small children. The need of her children, however, was stronger than the paralysis in her legs. Slowly she got up; painfully she walked into the next room and, taking her children by the hand, walked with them out of the house. Being a mother in a time of danger gave her a sense of mission that was strong enough to overcome her limitations.

And so, Christ comes into our lives—lives that are crippled and handicapped in so many ways. He gives us a purpose in life and He believes we can fulfill that purpose, and His belief becomes a magic force that makes weak men strong, failing men triumphant, and bad men good.

ELIMINATE THE WORD IMPOSSIBLE

Take another glance at Peter. He was a man of strange contrasts when Christ first met him. Sometimes he showed great courage.

For example, that night in the garden of Gethsemane Peter drew his sword and stood up against an entire company of soldiers. Yet later the same night, when a girl asked him if he were a friend of Christ, he cursed and denied it vigorously. He had great ideas and wanted to do big things, but really in his heart he was a coward. But Christ kept believing in him, and gradually Peter became a changed man.

Later on, Peter was arrested for preaching Christ and was put in prison. The next day in court Peter spoke courageously in his defense. There was no quivering, no fear, no hesitation about him. He had become as solid as a rock, even as Christ said he would. And then we read this thrilling sentence: "Now when they saw the boldness of Peter and John, and perceived that they were unlearned and ignorant men, they marvelled; and they took knowledge of them, that they had been with Jesus" (Acts 4:13).

One of the greatest mistakes we make is to think that if we could just solve some particular problem, or change the outward circumstances of our lives, we would be happy. That is not true. The place to change is inside ourselves.

Let me sugggest a simple exercise for one week. On the first day, keep a record with pencil and paper of how many times you say or even think the word, "impossible," or have kindred thoughts such as, "It is hopeless," "I can't do it," "It's too big for me," etc. Just before you go to bed check up on the number. The next day, keep a record again and concentrate on reducing the number of times you think a defeating thought. And so on through the week. It is marvelous what you can do for yourself. But because we are weak, let's take Christ into this with us; remember His words, "If thou canst believe, all things are possible to him that believeth" (Mark 9:23).

As a man yields his life to Christ, gradually Christ takes possession of him. St. Paul said, "Let this mind be in you, which was also in Christ Jesus" (Philippians 2:5). As He takes possession of our minds, we think as He thought. We eliminate the word, "impossible," from our vocabularies. We begin to believe and to act on our beliefs. Then a marvelous force begins to express itself in our lives; it is the magic of belief.

17.

LOOK AT SOMETHING BIG

HERE IS ONE of the grandest verses in the Bible: "When I consider thy heavens, the work of thy fingers, the moon and the stars, which thou hast ordained..." (Psalm 8:3).

Have you ever wondered why God made the world so beautiful, so impressive, so big? Nobody knows how big the heavens are with their millions, maybe billions, of stars. God didn't have to make it that big in order for the earth to exist. Why did God make it so that every morning the glory of a sunrise would come over the earth and every evening the quiet beauty of a sunset? He could have arranged it so the day would come and go in some less impressive manner.

Have you ever looked at a great mountain range and wondered why God made those high peaks? God could have left the mountains out of His creation. Mountains aren't really good for anything. They can't be cultivated; and beyond a certain point, they don't even grow trees. We do not need mountains in order to live on this earth.

I have flown across the trackless deserts of the West. As I looked at the endless miles of hot sand, I wondered why God made them that way. The deserts aren't good for anything. No food can grow there; the few creatures who live there are worthless to mankind.

Most impressed am I when I look at the ocean. Nobody really knows how big the ocean is. In places it is literally miles deep. It seems an awful waste. God could have fixed His creation so that rain could come without creating that vast reservoir of water. Why did He make the ocean?

God had a reason for making oceans, mountains, skies, and deserts. He never wastes anything. The Psalmist said, "When I consider thy heavens. . . ." The tragedy is that many people live amid God's creation and never consider it. A thoughtless person once said to Helen Keller, "Isn't it awful to be blind?" She replied, "Not half so bad as to have two good eyes and never see anything."

I like the reply of the boy who, when someone rebuked him for saying "I seen," replied, "It is better to say 'I seen' and see something, than 'I saw' and never see anything."

We have a little dog at our house. His entire world is our backyard. He has never even noticed the sky. The only time he ever looks up into a tree is if he is trying to catch a squirrel that has climbed out of his reach. He knows us and likes to be with us, but if anyone else comes into his yard, he barks at them and resents their presence. God's wonderful creation is wasted as far as our little dog is concerned.

And there are people who are content with a mighty small world. They never "consider the heavens." They never really see anything big.

When I think of the marvelous creation of the Lord—

the skies and seas, mountains and deserts—and wonder why God made it all, two answers come to my mind.

OUR GOD IS A GREAT GOD

The Psalmist says, "The heavens declare the glory of God" (19:1). The last time I was in New York I stood on top of the Empire State Building. I realized that whoever planned and built a building that big and high had big ideas, great abilities and resources. Little people could not have built it; they would not even have thought of it.

When you look into the face of the sky and consider something of its infinite size, you realize that no little God created it. He had to have big ideas and unlimited abilities. Truly we come to realize, "Our God is a great God." Realizing His greatness, we are not as afraid of what might happen in His world. Hitlers come and go, but they cannot defeat God. Our troubles seem hard to bear, but nothing can defeat the will and purposes of the Eternal Father.

I have watched colossal storms roar across the mountains. Heavy clouds come thundering in and everything gets dark. You begin to wonder if the world isn't going to be destroyed. Then, the clouds break up and you see the green mountainside bathed in sunlight. And you know that if you wait out the storm, there will be sunlight again. When we have trouble and everything seems lost, with a picture of the greatness of God in mind, we gain courage and calmness.

On the other hand, when the sun is shining and the

breezes are gentle, we know it will not always remain so. Sooner or later it will cloud up and rain again. So we make preparation during the good weather for the bad that is sure to follow. Likewise, when we are blessed with a life that is smooth and good, we remember that we must be ready for the trouble that is sure to come.

Realizing the greatness of God, our minds are stretched to take the long view of life, not living for just the moment but considering the whole. It has been determined by Greyselinck, the geologist, that if a movie of the entire history of the earth were made, and if the film ran for twenty-four hours, the first half of it would show history that man knows nothing about. In the twenty-four hour film, the life of man on earth would consume only the last five seconds of the film.

Such truth leads one to think in terms of eternity. A father whose son was recently killed said to me, "I could not bear it, if I thought this was the end of my boy. But God has planned far beyond this life and one accident will not wreck His plans."

Such truth keeps one from surrendering to troubles, because all troubles are momentary. It makes us realize that, come sunshine or storm, life goes on toward the accomplishment of God's purposes. Nothing can defeat Him. He is greater than all His creation.

To Think Big Thoughts

"When I consider thy heavens . . ." said the Psalmist. The Bible ties man in with the bigness of nature. God endowed man with the capacity to "consider" His wonderful creation. He did it for a reason. When you meditate on the bigness of skies and seas, mountains and plains, it causes you to think big thoughts. And when you begin to think big, you begin to act big.

I was preaching in another state recently. One night after a service, the pastor began to tell me of one of their ministers who had gone wrong. He mentioned the man's name and suddenly I was cold all over.

One night soon after I had begun my own ministry, I went to preach in a little country church. I got there early and was sitting on the steps waiting for the people to come. The first one to arrive was a young man. He sat down beside me and we sat there looking at the stars and talking about how they came to be. Then I called him by name and said, "God made you, too," and we talked about his life.

At the close of my sermon that night, that young man came forward, put his hand in my hand and his life in God's hand. He felt the call to the ministry. He responded to Him who said, "Go ye into all the world and preach the gospel." He worked hard and made a good beginning, but somewhere along the way, he began to look down and lost his vision. I don't know where he is now, but I am making every effort to find him. I believe I can persuade him to look with me again into the heavens. I believe I can bring new hope to his little broken-hearted wife. And I believe God will give him another chance and that he can still make good.

It has been said:

> Two men look out through the same bars:
> One sees mud, and the other sees stars.

God put the stars there hoping we will look up and

look big at life. When you see big things—like heavens, mountains, and oceans—you think big thoughts. And when you think big thoughts, your life begins to grow and you rise above a multitude of little things that would hurt you.

When Glenn Clark was a little boy, he had a nurse who foolishly tried to frighten him into being good. She told him that if little boys acted badly and didn't say their prayers, they would go blind and would not be able to see. After he went to bed and the light was turned off, he would begin to wonder if he could still see. So he would slip out of bed, go over to the window to see if he could see the stars.

"When I consider thy heavens. . . ." Some people become blind to the great things of God. Wrong living has a way of obscuring our vision. Neglect can also destroy our power to "consider the heavens." Maybe right now it would be well for you to stand before the window of prayer, and look again into the face of the Father.

18.

JESUS' FORMULA
FOR PEACE OF MIND

ONCE A YOUNG MAN made a list of the things he would like to possess in life. He listed health, love, beauty, talent, power, riches, and fame. He showed his list to a wise man much older in years. After reading the list, the older and wiser man replied: "An excellent list, well digested in content and set down in not-unreasonable order. But it appears, my young friend, that you have omitted the most important element of all. You have forgotten the one ingredient, lacking which, each possession becomes a hideous torment, and your list, as a whole, an intolerable burden."

"And what is that missing ingredient?" the young man asked.

With a pencil the old man crossed out the young man's entire list. Then, underneath he wrote down just three words—peace of mind. The young man was Joshua Liebman who later wrote the book, *Peace of Mind,* which has sold more than a million copies. In fact, there have been many books written on that subject and all of them have had large sales. Because more than any other thing—even health, power or riches—we want peace of mind.

But you do not need to read a book to find the pathway to peace of mind. Jesus summed the entire matter up in just eleven verses, Matthew 6:24-34. Notice the basic principle He sets forth: "No man can serve two masters: for either he will hate the one, and love the other; or else he will hold to the one, and despise the other. Ye cannot serve God and mammon."

The principle is clear: a divided mind is fighting against itself and thus it cannot be at peace. Your inner war must be ended by your complete, wholehearted decision. While life demands many decisions, Jesus would have us realize that basically there is just one decision. Settle that one and you settle them all. The decision is: God or mammon. The word mammon represents the desires of our body, and God represents the longings of our soul. Make up your mind which is most important and give yourself wholly to it. Then you will have peace of mind.

On one occasion Jesus said, "Remember Lot's wife" (Luke 17:32). He might have reminded us of her in connection with this most basic of all decisions, because she is a perfect example of indecision. As a member of a family that gave us our greatest prophets and purest saints, she had within her the faith of her family. She knew God, and from her childhood she had known the meaning of prayer.

But along with her husband she moved into Sodom, the city of mammon. More important, Sodom moved into her. She wanted God, but she also wanted Sodom. Finally the day of final choice came. She made a start toward God, but she looked back toward Sodom. Reaching for the stars with one hand and fingering the mud with the other, she revealed her divided heart, and she ended with misery and eventual destruction.

We must make the choice—"Ye cannot serve God and mammon."

What is the most complete picture of restlessness to be seen? I think it is the sea. Again and again I have stood upon the seashore and watched the constant movements of the sea. I have never seen it still, even for one moment.

Ceaselessly the ocean tosses itself upon the shores and then runs back again. Why can't the sea lie down and be still? Because it is the victim of a divided mind. The voices of the sky are calling to it. The ocean is drawn upon by the magnets in the heavens. But the muddy old world holds on and demands, "Stay with me." The ocean can never completely decide, and neither can it stop its ears to the voices it hears from the earth and from the heavens. Thus it is always tossing; it never finds rest and peace.

So it is with me and with you. Jesus said, "No man can serve two masters." Until you choose your master, you will never have peace of mind. There are two forces within every person struggling to become the master. One is his ideals, the call of the high life, the desire to be good and godly. The other is his selfish desires, his worldly nature. Goethe said it is regrettable that nature made only one man of him when there is material aplenty for both a rogue and a gentleman. We may choose the low life, but even then we will not have peace because God will never leave us alone. It is as Augustine said, "Man is restless until he finds his rest in Thee, O God."

COMMITMENT

Consider the picture of our Lord when ". . . he stedfastly set his face to go to Jerusalem . . ." (Luke 9:51). He heard the voice of inclination; He heard the voice of God. There was no wavering. ". . . he stedfastly set his face." Three elements made up His decision. First, there was commitment. There was no longer any question. The issue was settled. We need to deal honestly, even ruthlessly, with ourselves at this point. It is so easy to drift along without fully making up our minds. And most of our troubles grow out of indecision.

Have you read the book, *Quo Vadis?* The title means, "Whither goest thou?" Peter had failed to convert the

Romans and he determined to leave the city. On his way out, Christ appeared to him and said, *"Quo vadis?"* The question made Peter realize he was turning away from the work he had been called to do. So he turned around and went back, even though it eventually meant a martyr's death. But the main point is, Peter found the peace going back that he lost running away.

COURAGE

Out of commitment comes the second element, courage. Had you looked into the Lord's face as He turned toward Jerusalem, you would have seen no fear. It has been pointed out that we do not run because we are afraid; rather we are afraid because we run. Face up to it squarely and honestly; refuse to run. An old ship captain shouted to his sailors during a heavy storm, "Keep her facing it, always facing it, that's the way to get through." With decision comes courage.

". . . he stedfastly set his face to go to Jerusalem." He made the commitment and then as a result came courage. The two go hand in hand. We are afraid only until we fully decide.

CALMNESS

As a result of commitment and courage, something else comes—calmness. Even as Christ hung upon the pain-drenched cross, He spoke a calm valedictory: "Father, into Thy hands I commend my spirit" (Luke

118

23:46). I know of no other way to attain calm peace in our own minds and hearts.

Very often I get in an airplane to go somewhere. I always go through the same mental routine. When I sit down and fasten the seatbelt, I begin to wonder if this plane will fly. The engines start and I listen to see if they are running smoothly. Slowly the plane begins to move down the runway. The pilot can stop and go back until he reaches a certain point. That point is where the speed is so great that he couldn't stop; he must go on. It is the point of commitment. Then I settle down because there is no turning back. I must put my faith in the plane. And because I believe in the plane, I am not afraid and I feel calm as we fly into the sky.

Several years ago Joshua Liebman wrote *Peace of Mind*. Later Fulton J. Sheen wrote *Peace of Soul*. Since one of those was a Jew and the other a Catholic, the publisher suggested to Ralph W. Sockman, a Protestant, that he write on the same theme. He did write the book —entitled, *How to Believe*. I think he showed keen insight, because when one learns to believe he finds peace of mind and soul.

Because I believe in the airplane, I am willing to commit my life to the principle that it is able to carry me safely on my journey. Likewise, when I believe in God, I commit my life into His hands, believing that He can and will carry me through. And believing in God, being committed to God, I find courage and calmness. So Jesus said, "No man can serve two masters." Make your commitment.

Then read what Christ says following that verse: "Therefore I say unto you, Take no thought [be not anxious] for your life . . ." (Matthew 6:25). He points out that we do not need to worry about clothes, food, and the material things of life. Look at the birds of the air and the lilies of the field. God abundantly provides for them; shall He not do much more for one of His own children?

Jesus concludes by saying, "But seek ye first the kingdom of God, and his righteousness . . ." (6:33) Put God first. Decide once and for all on the right. Now notice— Christ doesn't say we will be denied the things we want in life. He says, ". . . all these things shall be added unto you" (6:33). The picture we have that the godly life must be one of hard sacrifice is wrong. The Psalmist said, "[I have] not seen the righteous forsaken . . ." (37:25). Come to think of it, I never have either. Have you?

19.
THE PEACE HE GIVES

ONE OF THE MOST appealing verses in the Bible is this one: "Peace I leave with you, my peace I give unto you: not as the world giveth, give I unto you. Let not your heart be troubled, neither let it be afraid" (John 14:27).

It makes us feel fine just to read that verse. Right now read it again. We feel drawn to those words as a thirsty man is drawn to a cool spring. More than anything else in this life we want inner peace. We are tired of living with our inner conflicts, tension, and turmoil; and we would rather possess peace of mind and heart than anything else.

Peace is not something we search for and work for. Jesus said, "my peace I give unto you." He gives it freely. All that remains is for us to accept it. But in order to be able to accept His peace, there are three other things we must accept from Him—His pardon, His Presence, and His purposes. Let's look at each of those.

His Pardon

First, we must accept His pardon. We have in mind some sin we have committed, some wrong of which we are ashamed. A sense of guilt haunts us, and we are never able to get away from it. We are sorry for what we have done, we refuse to do it again, and sincerely we ask God to forgive us. God always forgives those who ask Him to and who really mean it. We remember the Bible says, "If we confess our sins, he is faithful and just to forgive us our sins, and to cleanse us from all unrighteousness" (I John 1:9).

But there is a curious quirk within the human mind that makes it hard for us to accept God's forgiveness. Knowing we have done wrong, we feel we deserve punishment, and we live in constant dread and fear that something bad is going to happen to us. Subconsciously we say, "I've done wrong and someday I will pay for it." I went to the dentist the other day. He didn't hurt me, but I kept expecting him to any moment. Thus I could never relax as long as I was in his chair. And the constant dread and fear of some dire punishment for our sins robs life of all chance of deep inner peace.

121

Well, one way to gain faith in the forgiveness of God is to practice forgiving other people. In fact, this is essential because Jesus said, "For if you forgive men their trespasses, your heavenly Father will also forgive you ..." (Matthew 6:14).

In his book, *Learning to Have Faith,* Dr. John A. Redhead imagines a man with two buckets, one filled with water and the other with oil. Both are full to the brim. You cannot pour the oil from one bucket into the other because both are full. Also, the two would not mix.

Now, imagine that one of those buckets is you and the other is God. He wants to pour His forgiving love into your life, but you are holding resentment toward some person and thus you have no room for God. Also, God's loving mercy and your unforgiving spirit won't mix. So before you can accept His forgiveness, you must forgive that other person.

"My peace I give unto you," said Christ. Before you can accept His peace, you must first accept His pardon.

Some have come to me in a hopeless condition, feeling they have committed some unpardonable sin. I explain that the only unpardonable sin is to become so hardened by sin that the soul loses its feeling. The very fact that one feels a sense of guilt is positive proof of his ability to receive pardon. So I suggest to such a person that instead of concentrating on his sins, he fill his mind with God's promises to forgive his sins. Note these words:

"... Him that cometh to me I will in no wise cast out" (John 6:37) ; "... whosoever believeth in him should not perish, but have everlasting life" (John 3:16) ; "As far as the east is from the west, so far hath he removed our transgressions from us" (Psalm 103:12) ; "And Jesus said unto her, Neither do I condemn thee: go, and sin no more" (John 8:11).

Fix those words in your mind—"Him that cometh" . . . "Whosoever" . . . "removed our transgressions from us" . . . "sin no more." Those are God's words to you—accept His forgiveness and believe that you have received it.

His Presence

Second, to accept His peace, we must accept His Presence. At the beginning of World War II in England, the authorities evacuated the children from the areas under bombardment. But they soon discovered their mistake. The children became emotionally upset. Though they were safe, and all their physical necessities were provided for, being deprived of the love and companionship of their parents did them great harm.

So it is with us. We may live in the finest house, eat the best food, and have all the things money can buy. Still, without the fellowship of our heavenly Father, we remain restless and without inner peace.

The Bible says, "Be still, and know that I am God" (Psalm 46:10). Also ". . . in quietness and in confidence shall be your strength . . ." (Isaiah 30:15). Stillness— quietness: that is the greatest need of multitudes in the noisy, hurrying life of today. Note an amazing statement of Starr Daily, a man who knows much about the art of spiritual healing. He said, "No man or woman of my acquaintance who knows how to practice silence and does it has ever been sick to my knowledge."

Surely the practice of silence is more soothing and

healing than most medicines. How can one learn the art of stillness, of quietness, of silence? Pascal, the great scientist, said: "After observing human kind over a long period of years, I came to the conclusion that one of man's great troubles is his inability to be still."

I was on a plane once when the pilot announced over the speaker, "I am now going to cut the motors momentarily to make an adjustment to allow us to climb higher." To climb higher, man needs to learn to "cut his motor" and to make adjustments.

The Bible says, "Be still, and know that I am God." There is tremendous power to be gained from completely silencing the mind, but it isn't easy to do. Here is one way to accomplish it:

Go alone to the quietest place available to you. Do not read. Do not write. Begin by letting a mental picture of the most peaceful scene you have ever witnessed pass across your mind. Some months ago, I spent two weeks at Sea Island. Under the spell of that lovely place, every bit of the tension and hurry of life was drained out of me and I became completely relaxed. But for me, the benefits of Sea Island are not limited to the actual days I was there. I enjoy that experience again and again as I sit quietly and begin to see in my mind the ocean, the waves rolling up on the beach and back again, the gentle swaying of the sea grass. Through the power of imagination, one can quickly transport himself back into a peaceful scene and experience its healing influence.

Then, under that spell, begin to repeat audibly some peaceful words. Words have great suggestive power. Speak words like earthquake, murder, house on fire, cancer, blood—and you feel nervousness. But words like tranquility, serenity, imperturbable—such words create within you the mood they describe. Repeat them aloud, slowly and thoughtfully.

Have you ever dropped a pebble into a very still pond and watched the tiny waves go out over the surface of the water? Now while your mind is quiet, drop into it some of the great truths of God from the Bible, such as: "The Lord is my shepherd; I shall not want" (Psalm 23:1); "Let not your heart be troubled: ye believe in God, believe also in me" (John 14:1); "The eternal God is thy refuge, and underneath are the everlasting arms ..." (Deuteronomy 33:27).

Usually in this moment some lines of some of the songs I love will come to mind:

> What a friend we have in Jesus,
> All our sins and griefs to bear. . . .
>
> Jesus calls us, o'er the tumult
> Of our life's wild, restless sea,
> Day by day his sweet voice soundeth,
> Saying, "Christian follow me'.

His Purposes

Then, realizing God's pardon and experiencing His Presence, you take the third step necessary to the acceptance of His peace: You accept God's purposes. One of the primary causes of inner tension is mental disorganization. We have not learned to take up one thing at a time and concentrate on that. And above the daily routine of life, we have no guiding goals and purposes.

We remember the experience of the Master in Gethsemane. He got away from the crowd, even away from his closest friends. He got quiet and alone with God and then He said, ". . . nevertheless not my will, but thine, be done" (Luke 22:42). And who doubts but that in that moment all the inner strain and tension left Him. It is truly written, "In His will is our peace."

20.
WHAT CAN I BELIEVE ABOUT LUCK

Is THERE SUCH a thing as luck? Of course there is. Read Jesus' story of the Good Samaritan. A man was left wounded and half dead on the side of the road. Then Jesus said, "And by chance there came down a certain priest that way" (Luke 10:31).

"By chance"—a lot of things in your life happen by chance. You did not plan it; no one planned it—it just happened. It was pure and simple luck. Luck may be good or it may be bad—it is something that happens that was not planned or designed and could not be foreseen. And one of the bewildering facts of life is that many of the important happenings in our lives seem to come by chance or luck.

When I was a student at Wofford College in Spartanburg, South Carolina, my entire life was changed just by chance. I had a job for the summer in New York. Then I was going to the School of Religion at Duke the following year. It was all fixed. Just about a month before school was out, a man in New Jersey, the father of one of our ministers in North Georgia, died.

Because of the sudden death of his father, it was necessary for this minister to give up his work and go back home to meet the emergency. This left a church without a pastor, and to fill the vacancy several moves had to be made. Finally they had one little church left. Someone happened to mention my name to the district superintendent. He wrote offering me the church. I took it. I didn't go to New York. That fall, I went to Emory. I have often wondered what my life would have been if a man in New Jersey had not died suddenly. Or if he had died a month earlier or a month later. It was just chance—but my entire life will always be different because of it.

How did you meet your wife or your husband? I was talking to a couple the other day who told me they met on a blind date. Neither of them planned it—it was just luck. You probably met the one you married by luck. (Remember, there is both good and bad luck.) Some people say you are destined to marry just one particular person, but the fact is you could have married one of many and been just as happy. I heard about a husband who was so devoted to his wife that when she died, he had printed on her tombstone, "The light of my life is gone out." But about six months later, he met another woman and happily married her. Whereupon someone wrote on his first wife's tombstone, "But he struck another match."

In his book, *Christ the Truth,* Archbishop William Temple tells about a man walking down the street. A sudden gust of wind blew over a chimney on a house;

one of the bricks hit the man on the head and killed him. The wind had blown against that chimney many times, but this particular wind happened to blow it over and this man happened to be walking under it at that particular second. You cannot explain a thing like that except by saying it was pure chance or luck. If the man had been a second earlier or later he would not have been hit.

Many of life's most important happenings come by luck or chance. But that doesn't mean that life is determined by luck. Rather is your life determined by your reaction to your luck. Luck can either ruin us or make us—it depends not on our luck, but on us.

Two Things to Know

(1) Luck will ruin your life if you count on it instead of on careful preparation and hard work. One of the temptations of life is to go lazily along waiting for something good to happen—believing what is to be will be, no matter what we do about it. That attitude kills your soul and makes you a careless, shiftless person. As you go through life, you may run into good luck but let this be remembered: You won't run into anything if you aren't running.

Matthew Arnold said it well:

> We do not what we ought;
> What we ought not, we do;
> And lean upon the thought
> That chance will bring us through.
> —*Empedocles on Etna*

(2) Luck will ruin your life if you use it as an alibi for your failures. We have a way of excusing ourselves by saying, "That's just my luck." When you say that, you become blind to your real self. You do not see your own failures, and thus you do not feel inspired to improve yourself. Blaming defeat on luck causes you to sit back and accept it.

When you go to a football game, you see some player take a hard fall. But he never just sits in the middle of the field bemoaning his bad luck, saying, "Why did this happen to me? What have I done to deserve this? Why did I have to be the one who got hit?" Instead, he gets up and gets back into the game.

On the other hand, the existence of luck or chance in life can bring out faith and courage within us. You never develop faith unless you are willing to take a chance, and if all life were a sure thing, you would have no need for faith. The fact that you are willing to dream and dare in spite of the element of chance develops your character.

The farmer plants his crop in the spring. He spends money on seed, fertilizer, and labor, yet he is taking a chance on the weather. He may lose everything if there is too much rain or too little rain. In one sense, he is a gambler; but in another sense, he is very different from the gambler at a card table or a dog race. The gambler at a card table is destroying his character by counting on luck, while the farmer develops his character by his efforts to overcome the elements of chance. One is trying to get something for nothing. The other is paying the price and daring to risk his efforts because of his faith.

When a mother loves her child, she is taking a chance. That child may later break her heart, but the element of chance is what creates real love. This life cannot be lived on the basis of everything being certain and sure. Those who rise to life's heights are those whose faith and love grow bigger than anything that might happen.

But something else must be said about luck. The Bible says, "Be not deceived; God is not mocked: for whatsoever a man soweth, that shall he also reap" (Galatians 6:7). This is a law-abiding universe, and life will not ultimately be unjust. In the end, it all works out—not according to luck, but according to the laws and purposes of Almighty God.

While we know that much happens in life by luck or chance, we also know that this is a law-abiding universe and nothing happens that can defeat God and His purposes. We sometimes say, "Anything can happen," but that is a mistake.

Not everything can happen because God has kept His hand on this world and on our lives. As we see in the illustration of a child in its nursery, the parents do not cover the floor with a featherbed—thus, in learning to walk, the child may fall on the hard floor and hurt itself. This is part of the process of learning to walk. By putting the child in the nursery, the parents in a sense make it possible for the child to fall.

But on the other hand, the parents take certain precautions. They do not put razor blades or carbolic acid within reach of the child. Beyond a certain point, the child is protected. So has God dealt with His children on earth. Some things can happen, but God has so arranged it that nothing can happen that man cannot use for definite gain.

God has a plan and a purpose for every life. Something may break into that plan, but if I am faithful to

God, nothing can defeat it. If I put a big rock in the bed of a tiny stream, I stop its flow for a time, but soon the water finds a way around the obstruction and makes its way to the big river. So with life. There is always a way around our obstructions, and we can keep going until we get into the mighty river of God's eternal purpose.

Once I was in Talladega, Alabama, for a revival. While there, I visited the school for the deaf and the blind—the largest in the world. I sat in the classroom and watched the teachers patiently working with six- and seven-year-old children who were totally deaf. Never have I been so thrilled as I was when I saw how they were teaching those children to overcome their handicaps.

The school for the blind in Talladega has a band. One of the finest men there is the leader of that band. He, too, is blind. He leads by blowing a horn. When he was six years old, his eyes became infected. The physician gave a prescription; the parents had it filled and put it in the little boy's eyes. But there was a mistake—either the doctor made it, or the druggist, or the parents. Anyway, by chance or luck, he became blind. In spite of his blindness, he has become a wonderful man. And after all, wasn't that God's purpose for him? Who knows but that in overcoming his bad luck, he is now a better man.

When Judas died, a vacancy was left among the twelve disciples. Instead of waiting to find the best man, they cast lots. Matthias was selected. That place should have gone to St. Paul. It was mere luck that Paul missed it. But instead of being bitter, he went right ahead. No one ever heard of Matthias again, but Paul rose to a place of eminence. He didn't let a piece of bad luck spoil his life.

One thing more. In considering the things that happen by luck or chance, we must take the long view of life. After all, it doesn't matter whether I live in Atlanta or Houston, whether I am a preacher or a carpenter, whether I make a lot of money or a little. Read again the story of Dives and Lazarus (Luke 16:19-31). Dives seemed to have all the good luck and Lazarus the bad— but maybe it was the other way around. Dives' good luck blinded him to the really important things in life, and in the end he suffered for it.

In moments of good luck or bad luck, the main thing is to learn the purposes of God and not let our luck keep us from those purposes. It isn't your luck that really matters —it is what you do about it.

21.

WHEN OPPORTUNITY KNOCKS FOR THE LAST TIME

How many friends do you have? That is, how many do you have who will stand by you to the utmost and to the end? Who will keep on loving you and never let you down, no matter what happens? We sing, "What a friend we have in Jesus."

Other than that One who seeks to be the friend of every man, St. Paul had two such friends. One was Luke, "the beloved physician." Luke stuck with him when the last one had forsaken him. The other was Timothy, whom he called, "my own son in the faith" (I Timothy 1:2). It is believed by many that when Paul had been stoned by the mob at Lystra, dragged out of the city's gates and left for dead, it was Timothy who went out and found him after the mob had left, put his arms about his bleeding body, carried him to safety, and nursed him back to health.

Finally the great Apostle had about reached the end. He was in jail in Rome. Probably he would be executed. But even if he should be spared, his frail and tired body would not last much longer. He writes two letters to his friend, Timothy. They are kind and gentle and loving letters. Above all he longs to see him. He writes: "Do thy diligence to come shortly unto me" (II Timothy 4:9).

It is cold in that dreary jail. He remembers an old coat he had left in Troas. He asks Timothy to pick it up on the way and bring it. The hours go by slowly in jail, so he tells Timothy to bring him some books he had left, too. He comes to the end of the letter and he adds these words, ". . . come before winter."

Why "before winter"? Because when winter came navigation closed in the Mediterranean. If Timothy didn't come before winter, it would be too late. It was before winter or never. I wonder what Timothy did? I want to believe that he dropped everything and went. But on the other hand, he was busy. There was a church to be built in Ephesus, some elders to be ordained in Colossae, a series of services scheduled for Miletus.

He might have said, "I'll clear up these pressing matters first. Then, as soon as spring comes and the boats start running again, I'll go and spend a long time with my dear friend." If he took that course, when he landed in Rome, he rushed to the jail. But when he asked for Paul, the jailor said, "Why, they cut his head off three months ago. Every time the key turned in his jail door, he asked, 'Has Timothy come?' As we led him out that morning he looked down the road, but his friend never showed up."

On the other hand, I want to believe Timothy came "before winter" and walked by his friend's side down the jail's corridor that last morning. For all of us there come opportunities that must be taken "before winter." Put them off and it is too late.

There is an old saying, "Opportunity knocks but once." That is not true. Opportunity knocks many times. But it is true that opportunity has a way of knocking for its last time. "Come before winter," said St. Paul to Timothy. It was "before winter" or never.

Back in the year 1915, Dr. Clarence E. Macartney preached on the subject, "Come Before Winter". He repeated that sermon every year for forty years. Many wonderful results came from it. One night in Philadelphia, a medical student heard that sermon. The words, "Come before winter," kept ringing in his ears. He needed to study but first he wrote that letter to his mother he had been neglecting. He went out and mailed it.

The very next day, a telegram came telling him to hurry home. His mother was dying. It was a long trip and he finally got there. Under her pillow he found the letter he had written. It had meant so much to her. When he got back to Philadelphia, he thanked Dr. Macartney for preaching on "Come Before Winter."

Paul wasn't content merely to ask Timothy to come as soon as he could. He added "before winter." Timothy might forget there would come the time when it would be impossible to come. You know, we need that reminder—"before winter." I conduct many funerals and I find it is easier to speak words of comfort when loving friends have sent flowers. But sometimes I look at those flowers and wish they had come "before winter."

Dr. Macartney tells of a man who was under the bondage of liquor. One night he was in his hotel room; his craving came upon him; he reached for the phone for a bell boy. Suddenly he seemed to hear a voice. It was saying, "This is your hour. Yield now and it will destroy you. Conquer it now, and you are its master forever." Such moments come to every person. There are decision times and, once passed by, they are gone forever.

"Come before winter." Little boys and girls have a way of saying that. Every father plans on being a pal to his children. But young fathers need to get established in business; there is work to do. And golf, and dinner meetings, and the need to sleep past Sunday-school hour on Sunday, and this and that. Wouldn't it be wonderful if we could put our children in a deep freeze and keep them there until we had time for them? But children have a habit of growing up and getting away. If we love our children, it must be "before winter."

There is ill feeling between you and someone else. Maybe it is all his fault. Maybe it is yours. Maybe it is neither one's fault. Life is too short for that sort of thing. We mean to settle it, but we keep putting it off. Eventually it will have gone too far, or it will be too late. We need to settle it "before winter."

Whittier was right:

For of all sad words of tongue or pen,
The saddest are these: "It might have been!"
—*Maud Muller*, Stanza 53

The winter comes—opportunity has knocked its last time.

Isabella Braham told about receiving a thousand pounds unexpectedly. Immediately she gave a tithe, one hundred pounds, and wrote in her diary a revealing note about human nature, "Quick, quick, before my heart gets hard." The Bible speaks of giving "upon the first day of the week." I know people who intended to give, but they held on until they lost their willingness. "Come before winter!"

I am one who believes the church is important. It is important for the sake of the community. It is even more important for the sake of the individual members. But the only kind of church membership that means anything is active membership. During the years I have been pastor of a church, I have asked hundreds of people, "What church do you belong to?" Proudly they answer Baptist, or Methodist, or Presbyterian, or some other church. I have never met one person who was ashamed of belonging to some church. But I then ask, "What church in this city do you belong to?" And often, much too often, the answer is, "I haven't moved my membership." The years are slipping by. So many times my phone has rung and a tearful voice has said, "Will you conduct his funeral? He never joined a church here." "Come before winter!"

We remember how our Lord walked along the shores of Galilee and said to certain men, "Come, follow me." There must have been an urgency in His appeal because we read they "left all, rose up, and followed Him" (Luke 5:28). They did not wait. The appeal of our Lord is, "Come before winter."

Winter is a time when it gets cold. Instead of growing, the leaves on the trees turn brown and die. Winter also comes to the human heart. There are many decisions we must make "before winter," if we are to ever make them at all. Has winter come to your heart, as far as your love for God and your interest in Christ is concerned? Ask yourself some questions:

Do you say your prayers at night before going to bed as you used to? Does the singing of an old hymn give the same thrill it once did? Can you miss the services in your church without caring? Can you speak profanity without being shocked at yourself? The prophet Jeremiah said, "The harvest is past, the summer is ended, and we are not saved" (Jeremiah 8:20).

"Come before winter," Paul urged Timothy. If he waited, navigation would close down, there would be no boats running, and his chance would be gone. Yes— opportunity knocks many times, but eventually it knocks for its last time.

22.
WHY AND HOW TO READ THE BIBLE

To be perfectly frank, most people do not enjoy reading the Bible. And the fact is, most people do not read the Bible very much. This is true of both those in the church and those outside the church. It would be painfully embarrassing to poll a modern church congregation to find out exactly how much time each person gives to Bible reading.

Of course, we honor and respect the Bible. If the government were to pass a law forbidding us to read it, we would revolt. If some person makes a disparaging remark about the blessed Book, we resent it furiously. We take pride in possessing a copy, and most homes have several copies. We buy it in expensive leather bindings, and we all agree the Bible is the most important of all books. But still we must admit we don't read it very much.

Countless thousands of people have made a resolution to read the Bible all the way through, and some do, but most have found their enthusiasm failing by the time they finish Genesis. If they get through Exodus, Leviticus usually about ends the matter and the Bible is put carefully aside. Compared with television programs, the picture magazines, the romantic novels, and all the other things we have to claim our attention, most people find the Bible a rather dull and uninteresting book. Many who do read it regularly put it in the class of taking medicine—something we don't like, but we force ourselves to do it anyway.

When we do read the Bible, we get confused because we are reading about strange people and strange customs. They would go to war in the name of the Lord, they would sacrifice their babies on the altar, a man would work seven years to get his wife—today if a boy doesn't get engaged after his first few dates with a girl, he begins looking further. They did not have airplanes as we do; not even cars were invented back then—and it is hard to get excited about people who rode in ox carts. Well, why should we read the Bible?

The answer is found in the opening and closing words of the Book itself. It begins: "In the beginning God. . . ." Its final words are: "The grace of our Lord Jesus Christ be with you all. Amen." Through the sixty-six books of the Bible, there is one golden thread running that ties it all together just as thread holds together a string of beads. That thread is: there is a God, a God who takes an interest in the affairs of men, a God whose power is present in the life of man today.

The Bible contains God's revelation of Himself to man. I know people say they see God in the sunset, in flowers, in the lives of other people, in the study of history and in other ways, but without the revelation of God in the Bible, I doubt if we would see Him in any of those other ways. Without the Bible, man would be almost totally ignorant of God. If God matters, reading the Bible matters. So the important lesson to learn is how to read that Book so as to really get help from it.

Suppose you decide you would like to discover for yourself some of the treasures of the Bible. How should you begin? Would you start with Genesis and read all the way through Revelation? That would be the most unrewarding way you could read it. About all you would get out of that is just being able to say you had read the Bible through.

START WITH MARK

To really get help and find joy in your Bible reading, begin with Jesus. All that was written before Him was in preparation for His coming. All that was written after Him was to interpret His coming. There are four books in the Bible about Jesus, and by all means, the one to start with is St. Mark. Not only is it the shortest, it is also the most precious book the world possesses.

Get a picture of Mark in your mind. He was a boy in his early teens during Jesus' ministry. We think the Last Supper took place in his house. He saw the men slipping in that night, one or two together. He knew something was happening and, being a normal boy, he wanted to know what it was. He was not admitted into the room, but you may be sure he found a place where he could see and hear it all.

No doubt Jesus had visited Mark's home many times. Mark had come to know Him well, and to know Him was to love Him. He saw Judas leave, and it must have broken his heart. Teen-agers are usually disappointed when some adult lowers their ideals. Mark followed Jesus and the disciples into the Garden of Gethsemane. He heard the Master pray; he saw the soldiers take Him; he stood on the outskirts of His trials; he saw Him crucified. Most teen-age boys would have seen all that happen if they had been in Mark's place. Many believe it was Mark who said to the women that first Easter: "He is not here: . . . he is risen . . ." (Matthew 28 :6).

Probably Simon Peter was his hero. Of all the disciples, Peter was the one most likely to be chosen. Mark traveled with Peter, and in Rome he was probably impressed with the soldiers. Most boys get a thrill out of courageous action as typified by a soldier. He listened as Peter preached. As they traveled about, he would ask Peter about events in the life of Jesus. Being a young man, he was interested in action. Peter was also a man of action. So doubtless they talked more about what He did than what He said.

One day in Rome, Mark saw Peter put to death. Tradition has it that Peter made only one request, and that was that he be crucified with his head down. He did not feel himself worthy to be crucified in the same position as his Lord was crucified. Knowing Peter and his passion to preach Christ, it is likely that he made another request. "Mark," he may have whispered just before his death, "I won't be able to preach about Him anymore, but I have told you the facts. Before you forget, write the story of His life down and pass it around to the Christians to read."

After Peter was buried, Mark slipped away somewhere and wrote the story as he remembered it. By this time, Mark was about fifty years old, but he had not lost the enthusiasm of his youth or his love for the Lord. What he wrote makes mighty interesting reading.

THREE WAYS WE SHOULD READ

(1) *Read uncritically.* As long as I live I will never forget the first time I saw my wife. I might have said to her, "The earring on your left ear is crooked." I say, I might have said that, but I didn't. The truth is I did not notice whether she had on earrings or not. I don't remember whether she was wearing a red dress or a blue one. I didn't see all those details. I just saw her.

I'll never forget seeing the ocean for the first time. I just stood and looked at as much of it as my eyes could take in. I didn't stop to analyze the water to see if it had the proper mixture of hydrogen and oxygen, or to see how much salt it contained. I just looked at the ocean and my heart was lifted up by the very greatness of what I saw.

Turn to St. Mark's Gospel and look at Jesus like that. Don't worry about every little detail; don't stop on some verse that is hard to understand. Read those sixteen short chapters as you would read any other story. Don't argue about Him or try to reason with Him. Just take a good long look at Him through the eyes of Mark. Get the full picture in your mind first.

(2) *Read imaginatively.* Let your mind carry you back across the centuries and make you one of those who was actually present in the days of His life on earth. In the first chapter of Mark, you will meet John the Baptist —rough, fearless, truly great. Listen as his big voice booms out like the roar of a cannon: ". . . There cometh one mightier than I after me, the latchet of whose shoes I am not worthy to stoop down and unloose" (1:7). Does John sound as if he were talking about some pale-faced, anemic goody-goody who was weak and flabby? No. He was mightier than John. Let Mark draw the pictures for you, and one by one, let those pictures come into your view.

(3) *Read devotionally.* You are not seeking information when you read the Bible. You are seeking to meet a person. Recall that in John's Gospel, Jesus is quoted as saying, ". . . he that hath seen me hath seen the Father . . ." (14:9). Do you have questions about God? Someone has said, "I had a thousand questions until I met Him."

Suppose you were to sit down and write a description of the kind of God you wish we had. Describe His character and His activity just as you would like it to be. Then, as you read Mark's Gospel, you will find your own description expressed better than you did it yourself. Jesus was just what we want God to be. The best news ever given to man is that God is like Jesus. When the moment comes that you see God, it will be the most wonderful moment in your life. That is what we should get out of reading the Bible.

23.

GO DOWN DEATH

LET'S TALK ABOUT DEATH. Some protest. We do not want to hear the word "death" even mentioned. We prefer to go on pretending there is no such thing as death. We keep our age a secret and refuse to believe we are getting older. To maintain the illusion of eternal youth, we enlist the aid of health clubs, dressmakers, tailors, and beauty parlors. We buy creams and lotions, hair dyes and vitamin pills.

We recall that Job said, "If a man die, shall he live again?" (Job 14:14). We emphasize the "if" as though there were some doubt about whether or not a man dies. More properly we should say, "When a man dies." We try to disguise death with flowers covering the casket. We prepare a dead body to make it look lifelike. We dress the body in beautiful clothes and color pale cheeks —but the dead body is without any life. Dodge the fact as we will, death is real.

Some of us try to be nonchalant about death. We take the attitude of living today and not bothering about what lies beyond. Maybe nothing lies beyond, we say. Or if there is something else, we'll face it when it comes. That seems smart to some, to others it seems brave. Until —until someone I profoundly love has entered into that experience. Even if I am unconcerned about myself, I would hate to admit that I had grown so cold and in- different as not to love any other person enough to care. My child, my wife, my mother, my friend: when death comes to one of them, is it smart or brave for me to be nonchalant—*laissez-faire*—about death?

After the death of his wife, Arthur John Gossip preached: "You people in the sunshine *may* believe the faith, but we in the shadow *must* believe it. We have nothing else." Yes, now you may have a choice, but sooner or later comes a time when there is nothing else you can do but believe.

(1) Some refuse to think of death; (2) some are non- chalant about it; (3) others live in constant dread and fear of death. They read everything they can find on the subject, talk with all who will listen, but they cannot get the question off their minds.

(4) The Christian is also concerned about death, but with still a different attitude. Listen to the Christian sing: "We are marching to Zion, the beautiful city of God"; "I am bound for the promised land"; "There's a land that is fairer than day"; "When we've been there ten thousand years." For the Christian, death is not a mon- ster to be feared, it is a friend to be embraced.

The Christian believes in Him who said: "And whoso- ever liveth and believeth in me shall never die" (John 11:26); "In my Father's house are many mansions. . . . I

go to prepare a place for you. . . . that where I am, there
ye may be also. . . . because I live, ye shall live also"
(John 14).

Do you believe this?

James Weldon Johnson wrote a wonderful poem, "Go
Down Death." It came out of his childhood memories of
the sermons of the old Negro preachers. Death is an
angel in heaven—God is speaking:

And God said: Go down, Death, go down,
Go down to Savannah, Georgia,
Down in Yamacraw,
And find Sister Caroline.
She's borne the burden and heat of the day,
She's labored long in my vineyard,
And she's tired—
She's weary.
Go down, Death, and bring her to me

. . . .

While we were watching round her bed,
She turned her eyes and looked away,
She saw what we couldn't see:
She saw Old Death. She saw Old Death
Coming like a falling star.
But Death didn't frighten Sister Caroline;
He looked to her like a welcome friend.
And she whispered to us: I'm going home,
And she smiled and closed her eyes.

. . . .

Weep not, weep not,
She is not dead;
She's resting in the bosom of Jesus.

145

Peter Marshall, in his sermon entitled "Go Down Death," tells a wonderful story of a little boy with an incurable illness. Month after month the mother tenderly nursed him. But as the time went by, the little fellow gradually began to understand he would not live. One day he quietly said, "Mother, what is it like to die? Mother, does it hurt?"

Tears filled the mother's eyes and she fled to the kitchen to see about something on the stove. She knew the question must be faced. She leaned against the kitchen cabinet, her knuckles pressed white against the wall, and breathed a hurried prayer, "Lord, tell me how to answer him." And the Lord did tell her; immediately she knew what to say.

She returned to his room. "Kenneth," she said, "you remember when you were a tiny boy you used to play so hard, when night came you would be too tired even to undress, and you would tumble into mother's bed and fall asleep? That was not your bed—it was not where you belonged.

"In the morning you would wake up and find yourself in your own bed in your own room. Your father had come—with big strong arms—and carried you away. Kenneth, death is just like that. We just wake up some morning and find ourselves in the other room—our own room where we belong—because the Lord Jesus loved us."

The little lad never questioned again. Several weeks later he fell asleep just as she had said. That is what death is like.

And there is something else to be said. The pain and weakness caused by his illness was gone—forever. Some other things will be gone with death: endless processions of fears that have tortured someone's mind day and night; the drunkard's thirst, like the fires of hell; the bitter disappointments and the crushing pain of defeat; the tears of sorrow that shut out the sunlight; the deformed body; the broken dreams; broken hearts; and so many more things.

It is as John said, "And God shall wipe away all tears from their eyes; and there shall be no more death, neither sorrow, nor crying, neither shall there be any more pain: for the former things are passed away" (Revelation 21:4).

The Simple Story

What is it that takes the fear of death out of the mind of the Christian? It is Easter. Do not fail to hear the news as it is proclaimed. The same story is told over and over—it goes something like this:

A man by the name of Jesus once lived. One Friday He was crucified. After one of the soldiers had thrust a spear into His side to make sure He was dead, he probably turned away saying, "That one didn't take long." Simon Peter, one of Christ's followers, was heard to say, "I go a fishing." There was nothing else left to do. He had visions of Christ bringing in a Kingdom, but now He was dead. So it was back to the little boat with its patched sails, back to mending the nets.

Came Sunday morning. Three women had come to anoint His body. They found the stone rolled away and His tomb empty. Two of the women left. "But Mary stood without at the sepulchre weeping" (John 20:11). She saw a man but did not recognize Him. Then He said, "Mary." The way He spoke her name! No one else had said it as He had. Just that one word, yet all of heaven was in it. She cried, "Master!" She knew. There was no doubt. It was He.

That afternoon some friends of His who lived in Emmaus recognized Him by the way He broke the bread. That same night, ten of the disciples were together when He appeared to them. They never doubted again. Eight days later, He invited Thomas to ". . . Reach hither thy finger, and behold my hands; and reach hither thy hand, and thrust it into my side: and be not faithless, but believing." Thomas answered, "My Lord and my God" (John 20:27, 28).

Others saw Him, some through their physical eyes and others, like St. Paul, through the reality of a spiritual experience. They went everywhere telling about His resurrection. It wasn't a story they invented. Would any man have invented such a story in order to be crucified upside down, as was Peter? Or to get his head chopped off, as did Paul? Or to be stoned to death, as was Stephen?

The Bible says, "Then were the disciples glad, when they saw the Lord" (John 20:20). The Greek word here for "see" does not mean to look through your physical eyes, as you look at a mountain, or at another person, or at the words on a printed page. The word "see" here means inner sight—perception—understanding.

"When the disciples saw!" They were never afraid again—not even of death. Peter was to be executed one morning at daybreak. The night before he did not pace the floor of his cell as some wild animal might have. Instead, he calmly lay down and went to sleep. When they observed the change in those who "saw," their enemies "marvelled; and they took knowledge of them, that they had been with Jesus" (Acts 4:13).

We, too, stand before an open grave. We see One standing by. He calls our name. We can never explain it; we only know it is true. We "see" the Lord and we hear Him saying, "because I live, ye shall live also." And we know it is true.

24.

ETERNAL LIFE

WHY DO SO many more people go to church on Easter Sunday than any other Sunday of the year? It is because Easter is the firmest hold that man has on life after death.

In Thornton Wilder's play, *Our Town,* one of the characters says: "I don't care what they say with their mouths—everybody knows that something is eternal. And it ain't houses, and it ain't names, and it ain't earth, and it ain't even stars . . . everybody knows in their bones that something is eternal, and that something has to do with human beings. All the greatest people ever lived have been telling us that for five thousand years and yet you'd be surprised how people are losing hold of it. There's something way down deep that's eternal about every human being."

That is true—"Everybody knows in their bones that something is eternal." We do not have to have a reason to believe it. It is intuition with us. We just know it. Yet, ". . . people are losing hold of it." Into our minds come doubts. Sometimes the thought of death puts panic into our hearts. We associate death with shadows and with darkness.

"Sunset and evening star, And one clear call for me!" we quote. Or we sing, "Abide with me: fast falls the eventide; The darkness deepens; Lord with me abide. . . ."

On Easter, we take hold again of the certainy of eternal life. We look to that day to take away the gloom and the fear, to give us comfort and assurance. I know there are some people who claim not to be interested in the life beyond. A friend of Maude Royden's said:

> Don't bother me now,
> Don't bother me never;
> I want to be dead
> Forever and ever.

After I had conducted the funeral service for a dear mother her little boy, less than ten years old, said to me, "Where's my Mamma now?" I might have said, "She's dead," but that would have been a sorry answer. Yet— without Easter I would have had no other answer. We come to church that day because there is an answer. The answer is the promise of Christ, "Because I live, ye shall live also." You find those words in the fourteenth chapter of St. John (14:19).

He begins that chapter with: "Let not your heart be troubled . . ." and he goes on to tell that beyond this life there is another abiding place. He says He will be there and that we will be with Him. But is that true? Can you believe it? Is there any proof? "Because I live," He said. On the fact of His resurrection rests man's assurance of life after death.

150

On Easter Sunday, in more than a thousand languages, we sing and say, "Christ, the Lord is risen today." But is it really true? How can we be sure?

REASONS WE ARE SURE

You believe there once lived a man by the name of Jesus. You are familiar with much that He said and did—how He offered a new way of life, performed miracles, and loved people. You know that He was put to death, but do you really believe that He lived again after death? You can say, "Yes, I believe that he rose from the dead" and yet not realize it.

One of the truly great preachers was Dr. A. W. Dale of England. His books have meant a great deal to me, but he had preached for years about Christ before the truth really dawned upon him. Afterward he wrote: " 'Christ is alive,' I said to myself. 'Alive!' And then I paused: 'Alive!' Can that really be true? Living as I myself am? I got up and walked about repeating, 'Christ is living! Christ is living!' At first it seemed strange and hardly true, but at last it came upon me as a burst of sudden glory; yes, Christ is alive. It was to me a new discovery. I thought that all along I have believed it; but not until that moment did I feel sure about it."

How can we know, as Dr. Dale knew, that Christ is risen? There are two ways to know: (1) Through a study of the evidence; and (2) through an experience of His Presence. Our evidence is found in the last two chapters in each of the first three Gospels—Matthew, Mark, and Luke—and the last three chapters of John. He was pro-

151

nounced dead. His body was embalmed. Remembering that He said He would rise, every possible precaution was taken to prevent a hoax or a fake. His body was placed in a grave hewn in solid rock and sealed with a large stone. The stone was so large that three women together could not move it.

A Roman guard of the finest soldiers the world had known was stationed to watch His grave. Then an earthquake came. An angel descended from heaven. Because of their fear, these soldiers did shake and become as dead men. Later it was suggested they fell asleep, but you cannot imagine an entire company of Roman soldiers falling asleep on duty. The noise of the stone moving would surely have wakened some.

His own followers did not expect Him to rise. Not even one of them expected it. If they had thought it was even a possibility, they would have been waiting around His tomb instead of shutting themselves up in a room, with the doors barred for fear. Even when they were told the news, they did not believe.

In fact, it took forty days for the Lord to convince them. During those forty days He appeared to them seven times that we know of. And then He ascended out of their sight. I think there is no greater proof of His resurrection than the change that took place in those men who knew Him best.

When He was buried they were depressed, frightened, and filled with despair. Just seven weeks later, they were fearlessly shouting the news to every person who would listen. After Jesus ascended, they were men filled with joy and courage and with a vision of conquering the world in His name. The evidence of His resurrection was strong enough for those who were there.

Jesus said, "Because I live, ye shall live also." We can know that He lived through studying the evidence of His death and resurrection. But that is not sufficient. St. Paul never saw Christ in the flesh. He heard the stories of His resurrection. In the fifteenth chapter of First Corinthians, which incidentally is the greatest statement on life after death that has ever been made, he records the fact that:

After His resurrection, Christ ". . . was seen of Cephas, then of the twelve: After that, he was seen of above five hundred brethren at once; of whom the greater part remain unto this present, but some are fallen asleep. After that, he was seen of James; then of all the apostles" (15:5-7).

But for a long time Paul did not believe that preponderance of testimony. In fact, the stories of Jesus angered and upset him. To him the followers of Christ were fanatics, and Paul did all he could to put an end to their talk and activity. Then one day Paul watched as one of the Christians named Stephen was stoned. There was something in the way Stephen died that disturbed Paul. Stephen had something that Paul knew he didn't have.

And we, too, have seen this "something" in the lives of other people. We have observed in certain ones who profess to be Christians a radiance, a goodness, a quality of character and life that is different. We know of those who have sacrificed in the support of His work, and maybe we have wondered why they would do it. Yet even this does not completely convince us.

Finally St. Paul said, "And last of all he was seen of me

also, as one born out of due time" (15:8). As Paul made his way along the Damascus road, his conscience bothered him (Acts 9:1-6). He felt that he was not living the life he should. He wasn't easy in his mind about it. Suddenly light from heaven began to shine around him. Then a voice began to speak asking why he kept on rebelling and not doing what he knew he should do? Then Paul said, "Lord, what wilt thou have me to do?" Acts 9:6).

He surrendered his rebellious will. He began to live and do as he felt Christ wanted him to. From then on he lived for Christ. At the end of his life he was in jail and soon to be executed. But he was not worried. Instead, he wrote to his young friend Timothy and told him, "Fight the good fight of faith, lay hold on eternal life . . ." (I Timothy 6:12).

And today, as we "fight the good fight of faith," we come into a realization that Christ does live. We joyously sing: "He lives, He lives, salvation to impart. . . . You ask me how I know He lives? . . . He lives within my heart." And because we know He lives, we can say even as the great Apostle said, "O death, where is thy sting? O grave, where is thy victory? . . . thanks be to God, which giveth us the victory through our Lord Jesus Christ" (I Corinthians 15:55, 57).

25.

WHAT THE BIBLE SAYS
ABOUT HEAVEN

WHAT DOES the Bible say about heaven? Down through the centuries, man has wondered about heaven and wanted to know more about it. The Psalmist looked into the skies and was so impressed by them that he declared, "The heavens declare the glory of God . . ." (19:1).

In every possible way, mankind has sought answers to his questions about the heavens. We have built giant telescopes to pierce the outer spaces and space ships that lift one miles and miles above the earth. We have learned a lot about the lands of the sky, yet the heavens are still mysterious. We say with the poet, "Twinkle, twinkle little star, how I wonder what you are."

We know that no telescope can see the heaven we are most interested in, neither will any space ship ever be able to ascend to its pearly gates. The only reliable information we have about heaven is what the Bible says. I spent an entire evening recently reading in the Bible about heaven. When I got through, a lot of my questions were *not* fully answered.

We wish the Bible told us such things as: Will babies who die always be babies in heaven? Will old people who die always remain old? Will we see and recognize each other there? Will we miss people who are not there? What sort of activity goes on in heaven? What happens during the interval between leaving this world and arriving in the next? Even if we find the answers to these questions, we want to know more.

How big a place is heaven? Today approximately two billion people die every thirty years. When we think of all who have died since Adam and all who will die in the future centuries, could even the universe be big enough to hold them all? Do people in heaven know what people on earth are doing? Can they communicate with us? Could one come back to earth, if he wished to? I find no specific answer to any of those questions in the Bible, yet we find the answer to all our questions as we read the holy Book.

MAN IS NOT AT HOME ON EARTH

To begin with, we see in the Bible how God has put into man a restlessness in this world. The Psalmist said, "I am a stranger in the earth . . ." (119:19) and St. Paul declares, "We are . . . willing rather to be absent from the body, and to be present with the Lord" (II Corinthians 5:8). Man is essentially a spiritual being and can never be completely at rest in this world. An old song says,

I am a stranger here, within a foreign land;
My home is far away, upon a golden strand. . . .
I'm here on business for my king.

Something in man is always seeking a fuller life. Earth never completely satisfies him. Other creatures seem to fit into the world of nature, but man is constantly looking for something else. I spend a lot of nights in hotels, but it isn't like being at home. And the Bible tells us that heaven is our home, the end of the journey.

HEAVEN IS A PLACE PREPARED

What is heaven like? Jesus said, "In my Father's house are many mansions [rooms]" (John 14:2). How many is many? Some people have mighty narrow thoughts about it. They think heaven is a tiny little place reserved especially for them and a few people who think as they do.

The Bible tells us there are twelve gates opening in every direction (Revelation 21:12, 13) and streaming in through those gates is a multitude so great that no man can number them. They come from all nations and they are all kinds of people (Revelation 7:9). What a rebuke to our narrow prejudices and our selfish exclusiveness!

Also Jesus said, "I go to prepare a place for you" (John 14:2). Each person has a distinctive place both in the Father's heart and in the Father's house. You will still be you over there. When parents have a son who lives in another city and he is expected home for a visit, Mamma puts clean sheets on his bed, prepares the dinner she knows he will like, and does everything possible to make him happy at home. Likewise Christ says, "I go to prepare a place for you." It will be a place we will like.

Why did He not tell us more about that place? I think the reason is, if He had, it would at this time really not appeal to us. The Bible tells us that in heaven ". . . we shall all be changed" (I Corinthians 15:51). That is not surprising. We are constantly changing. When I was a little boy, the railroad ran in front of our house. I watched the big engines go by and wished I could ride with the engineer. That would have made me so happy. Once I was taking a train trip. I knew the engineer and asked if I might ride with him for a time. He let me, but I was disappointed. The experience that would have thrilled me so as a little boy now was dull for me.

Man has an amazing capacity for growth. He only begins to touch his possibilities here on this earth. In heaven are lifted the limitations of the flesh and we reach our highest and best selves. We think in terms of little pleasures here. We satisfy ourselves with earthly joys. But when we become fully developed we will have capacities to enjoy so much that we cannot even conceive of now. So we are told, ". . . Eye hath not seen, nor ear heard, neither have entered into the heart of man, the things which God hath prepared for them that love him" (I Corinthians 2:9). Jesus did not tell us more simply because we would not now understand or appreciate it. Sufficient is the fact that He is preparing for us—each one of us.

Since my wife and I have been married, we have lived in ten different houses. I don't remember how many chairs there were in any living room we ever had or the color of a single rug in any house we have lived in. I have never paid much attention to the furniture we had, but many nights I have driven across the state to get back to one of those houses. Why was I so anxious to get to that house? Because my wife was there and our children were there, and my loved ones being there is what made it home. And I want to know if we will be together in heaven.

We Will Know Each Other There

Will we know each other in heaven? That is the main question about eternity that we want answered. After the death of his wife, Robert Browning wrote his lovely poem, "Prospice," in which he said:

O thou soul of my soul! I shall clasp thee again,
And with God be the rest.

Just to clasp her again would have been heaven for him.

Charles Kingsley selected the words for his tombstone: *Amavimus, Amamus, Amabimus*—"We have loved, we do love, we shall love." The love of his life here, he did not expect to lose over there.

But this brings up complications. Some men asked Jesus, what if a woman were married several times, whose wife would she be in the resurrection? That question worries people today who have had more than one wife or husband. And the matter of family reunions in heaven is hard to understand. Will my wife be with her father and mother, and will I be with mine? Then what about our children and our family?

Jesus said that in heaven we "neither marry, nor are given in marriage . . ." (Matthew 22:30). The problem exists because we think in terms of physical relationships and heaven is on a higher plane. Love in heaven is not less real, but more real. Surely we will know each other there. The Bible doesn't directly discuss the matter of recognition in heaven; it just assumes it.

As Jesus talked with His disciples about the Father's

house, He said, ". . . if it were not so, I would have told
you" (John 14:2). Surely He who did so much to
strengthen human love on earth would have told us if we
are to lose that which is most precious to us.

As our Lord hung on the cross, He spoke to one dying
by His side. He didn't say, "Well, I hope to see you
again." Neither did He say, "We might see each other
again." He said, ". . . Today shalt thou be with me . . ."
(Luke 23:43). We are the same people over there.
Moses and Elijah had been dead for centuries when they
came back to visit with Christ on the Mount of Trans-
figuration. But they were still the same. We will love
each other again and all the problems we can think of
have already been solved.

I have no worries about heaven when I read John's
vision in Revelation 4:2, 3. He says, ". . . behold, a throne
was set in heaven, and one sat on the throne. . . . and
there was a rainbow round about the throne. . . ." A
throne signifies authority, law and order. Heaven is not a
place of chaos. On the throne is the Father and that
means His will is being done. Everything there is perfectly as it should be.

The rainbow means the storms are past; it is the sym-
bol of hope beyond the tragedies. Here on earth we have
troubles and heartaches, but there everything is all right.
On earth man has done his worst; over there God has
done His best—and nothing could be better than God's
best. God is on the throne with a rainbow round about—
nothing needs to be said beyond that.